Advance Praise for
The Moment That Defines Your Life

"In *The Moment That Defines Your Life*, Chuck Garci: about the life-changing power of emotional intellige: stoicism. Through captivating stories of individu: overcame adversity, he informs, inspires, and provi tools that integrate emotional intelligence and stoici cial to aid in your personal and professional transforr

— BOB LITWIN, Three-time Tennis World Champion and auth
the Best Story of Your Life

"Chuck Garcia is a rare individual who truly 'talks and climbs the climb!' Chuck doesn't simply tal Emotional Intelligence—*he lives it. The Moment Tha Your Life* presents the subject in a way that enable immediately implement these life-critical skills ir daily routine. This is the book...*if you're ready to cha life and ace every relationship*!"

— YITZCHOK SAFTLAS, Radio Show Host of 710 WOR *Mind You with Yitzchok Saftlas*

"Chuck is the rarest of authors. In *The Moment Tha Your Life*, he seamlessly cross-pollinates ideas from : emotional intelligence, mountaineering, and leade weave something that will keep you gripped until page. His brilliant insights are only superseded by l less execution of them in every moment of his life."

— SOUNDARYA BALASUBRAMANI, Author of *Unshackled* and *Admi*

The
MOMENT
THAT DEFINES
YOUR LIFE

The
MOMENT
THAT DEFINES
YOUR LIFE

Integrating Emotional Intelligence & Stoicism
when your Life, Career, & Family are on the Line

CHUCK GARCIA

SAVIO
REPVBLIC

A SAVIO REPUBLIC BOOK
An Imprint of Post Hill Press
ISBN: 978-1-63758-982-3
ISBN (eBook): 978-1-63758-983-0

The Moment That Defines Your Life:
Integrating Emotional Intelligence and Stoicism when your Life, Career,
and Family are on the Line
© 2024 by Chuck Garcia
All Rights Reserved

Cover Design by Cody Corcoran
Interior Graphics by 2MarketMedia

posthillpress.com
New York • Nashville
Published in the United States of America

1 2 3 4 5 6 7 8 9 10

The Moment That Defines Your Life is dedicated to Eric Skopec, my debate professor at Syracuse University. His course and extraordinary teaching style had more impact on me than any other in twenty years of formal education. No subject matter helped me better bridge the gap between college and career than his. I subsequently try my best every day to live up to the exceptional communication standards he inspired inside and outside the classroom.

CONTENTS

FOREWORD

Y ou've picked up a book about the moments that define you when your career, family, and life are on the line.

I faced such a defining moment a few years ago, which I could not have come through without the immeasurable patience and guidance of this book's author, Chuck Garcia.

Had I not met Chuck when I did, not only would I have lost everything, but I would also have seen everything as lost, and those are very different things. Loss is inevitable. How we see it is a choice.

Shortly after turning fifty, I was trapped (my view at the time) in the simultaneous collapse of both my twenty-five-year career as a screenwriter and my ten-year marriage. As I spiraled into feelings of failure, a friend suggested I speak with Chuck. What I skeptically projected would be a short phone call turned out to be a crossroads.

Chuck was embarking on an adventure of his own at the time, taking his A Climb to the Top coaching brand up a new mountain, literally, shooting a TV pilot in which he would guide four people facing defining moments in their lives to summit the 5,114 ft. of Algonquin Peak in upstate New York's Adirondack Mountains. Hearing how I was facing the upheaval of my entire world, Chuck invited me to be one of the cast members.

I had spent my film career behind the camera, so the idea of being in front of one was uncomfortable, but I also knew that this invitation was not one to brush off flippantly with the excuse of "too much going on."

So, two months later, I found myself on a mountain trail with Chuck and his hardworking young crew, beset by unexpected rain that had us hours behind on the climb. Filming a "check-in," I expressed my pain at how divorce might affect my six-year-old daughter and two-year-old twins and my doubts about whether I could even muster the kind of energy needed to build a new career from scratch at an age when many of my friends were looking toward retirement.

Chuck saw what I was too afraid to look at, that I had given up, buckled down for the storm of my life to pass, hoping for calm at the other end so that I could then find the strength to go on.

It was in that moment, on that mountain while trudging through actual rain and mud, that I realized it is *not* in the calm at the end of life's trials and challenges that we determine our paths. If you're just waiting for the storm to pass, your chance to choose your path through it *passes with it*, and you wind up wherever the storm will take you.

Our defining moments are found *within the storm*.

They swirl around us in waves and froth and lightning and rain, challenging us to find within ourselves not only the ability to recognize the moment for what it is but the strength to *define ourselves* within it, to choose our own path through rather than let the storm choose for us.

While my career, family, and life were certainly on the line, Chuck reminded me that as we venture into the world each day, our careers, families, and lives are *always* on the line. That we have a choice in each of those moments to go blindly through life hoping that tragedy never finds us (or finds us unprepared when it inevitably does) or that we can open our eyes and face it.

He opened my eyes...and I faced it.

Chuck poured these lessons into me with wisdom and care and Emotional Intelligence so deeply woven into his gentle presence, into his very being, that the Stoics he so fondly and reverently honors in this book would be proud.

Chuck *lives* the philosophy of inner peace through outer calling, self-service through the service of others, and success through the sacrifice of selfishness. I am forever humbled and grateful to be the recipient of his kind and generous example.

I'm happy to say that while my career, family, and life have all changed dramatically, I neither lost nor see as lost anything that has changed. To the contrary, I have learned to embrace and even enjoy the storm as much as the calm. (Thank you, Chuck, for that.)

It was through his coaching that I chose to also become a coach. I flew back to Los Angeles after our *A Climb to the Top* show, no longer dwelling in the perceived failures of my past but excited to create a new future for myself by helping others to create theirs—and I am fortunate to have now succeeded in both.

That's what Chuck is doing with this book.

You're about to be treated to many stories of the defining moments its subjects faced and the lessons they learned, too often through tragedy, though which those lessons likely could not have been learned had it not been for the tragedy.

You will see yourself in some of these stories.

You will see the best of humanity in all of them.

By the end you will have your eyes opened, their lids permanently propped up, scouring the storms for the defining moments that, if not looked for, can so easily pass us by, never seen or known for what they were or could have been; and when found...well, that is for each of us to discover.

I found mine on a mountainside in upstate New York.

Where will you find yours?

Ken Golde
Executive Coach
CEO, Breakthrough Leadership Training
Author, The F.A.S.T. Way: Defining and Expressing Yourself for Ultimate Success

INTRODUCTION

Not My Day to Die

*"Our greatness lies not so much in being able
to remake the world—that is the myth of the atomic age—
as in being able to remake ourselves."*
Mahatma Gandhi

On September 11, 2001, at 8:46 a.m., American Airlines Flight 11 crashed into the North Tower of New York City's World Trade Center, killing all passengers aboard and over one thousand people above the ninety-first floor. Sixteen minutes later, United Flight 175 smashed into the South Tower, killing everyone on the plane and hundreds more in the building.

Thirty minutes before these horrific attacks, eighty people were gathered at a restaurant/event space called Windows on the World to participate in a conference sponsored by a London-based organization called the Risk Waters Group. Located on the 106th floor of the World Trade Center's North Tower, one could see Manhattan's sparkling skyscrapers to the north, Brooklyn's beautiful bridges to the east, and the stately Statue of Liberty to the south. By 8:30 a.m., an additional seventy-two restaurant staff arrived before their breakfast service to further prepare for this two-day event. Add a handful of conference delegates who had just arrived, and over two hundred people were at Windows when the planes struck.

While planning this event in the summer of 2001, the conference producers scheduled me to speak on 9/11 at 9:20 a.m. and again on 9/12 at 11:00 a.m. On a follow-up call two months earlier to resolve a conflict with another speaker, they asked if I could move my 9/11 morning slot to 3:20 p.m. that afternoon. I was happy to accommodate the change, given another speaking engagement request I received a few days earlier.

Instead of being at the World Trade Center when the planes struck that morning, I was giving a speech at the Empire Hotel in Midtown Manhattan, approximately six miles away. With a 9:00 a.m. start, I planned to finish it in forty-five minutes, then take the subway downtown to spend the rest of the day at Windows on the World.

I indicated a few days before the conference on a calendar entry visible to all Bloomberg employees that I had a speaking engagement at the World Trade Center on 9/11/01 and would be there until 6:00 p.m. I made no reference to the Empire Hotel and never thought to enter an expected arrival time at Windows on the World.

During the Empire speech, I was interrupted at 9:20 a.m. by a conference producer who explained to me and the audience that a "hard to believe but alarming incident occurred a few minutes ago at the World Trade Center." He then directed the sixty of us to a television set tuned to CNN. Stunned at what we were watching, it was unimaginable! The higher floors in both towers were burning, smoke billowing, with no words to describe our shock. I had never seen anything like this. No one said a word as we witnessed the inconceivable. Occasionally someone let out a gasp as all eyes and ears were directed at the television set. We just stood still, unable to process what felt like a horror movie. The silence was deafening.

The Twin Towers of the World Trade Center (WTC) in New York City's Financial District were ablaze without explanation. There were rumors that airplanes struck the towers, but the newscasters hesitated to commit until a reliable source confirmed it. Little did we know that within the hour, an American Airlines plane smashed into the Pentagon in Arlington, Virginia, and a United Airlines jet crashed into an open field in rural Pennsylvania, killing everyone aboard. The combined death toll for all four incidents that day was 2,997.

Disorientated at the gruesome sight of the towers burning, all anyone could do was call their families, friends, and colleagues. However, landlines and cellular phones were not working. We were amidst the deadliest terrorist attacks in American history and had no means to communicate. I was frantic to speak with my family, who knew I was ending my day at the WTC, and the office, to let them know I was all right. Everyone in the hotel beat their phones in frustration, desperate to communicate with their loved ones. No go. We were out of contact with the world. In addition, all transportation citywide was halted. New York City was under siege and in lockdown. The South Tower subsequently collapsed at 9:58 a.m. Thirty minutes later, the North Tower crashed to the ground.

Since riding the subway to the World Trade Center was not an option, I walked from the Empire Hotel to Bloomberg's headquarters at 499 Park Avenue. Unbeknownst to many, I was alive. The first colleague I met when I entered the building said, "Chuck, everyone thinks you are dead. Walk the halls and let them know you are not. They may still be shaken but relieved." I didn't know it until then, but my name was on a list that implied unaccounted for and presumed dead.

Aware that my company calendar stated, "World Trade Center until 6," Bloomberg employees made a mental leap and concluded I was already at Windows on the World. My three colleagues Bill, Peter, and Paul had sent a text to the office after the planes hit, stating they "were trapped above the fire." Sadly, they perished when the North Tower collapsed. Bewildered by the day's unprecedented events, there was a feeling in the air that nothing would ever be the same. Who knew?

Over the next month, I attended sixteen memorial services as New Yorkers walked around the city in a fog, shell-shocked at the death and destruction. The Twin Towers, icons of the New York City skyline, were gone. It was painful to look downtown and see airspace where previously they loomed large over New York's Financial District. Day after day, I wondered what force in the universe decided who lived and died that day. Never was I so perplexed by an endless string of questions on the nature of human existence. For the next several days, carrying the weight of survivor's guilt, I was a ball of confusion. One question kept burrowing in my mind that I couldn't shake:

"Why was this not my day to die?"

With a phone call and a simple twist of fate, my speaking schedule at the World Trade Center changed from morning to afternoon on September 11, 2001. Were it not for the resolution of someone else's conflict, I would have died that day. Reflecting on this turn of events, I was suddenly jolted by that moment. In Viktor Frankl's classic *Man's Search for Meaning*, he states,

> *"Everything can be taken from a man but one thing: the last of the human freedoms—to choose one's attitude in any given set of circumstances, to choose one's own way...*
>
> *When we are no longer able to change a situation, we are challenged to change ourselves."*

Frankl's survival story at Auschwitz was running through my head every hour of every day. I couldn't shake it. The phrase "We are challenged to change ourselves" became foundational to turning crisis into opportunity.

As I reflected on the 9/11 events, I became the protagonist in my own story arc. Who could have predicted how this plot would develop? The entire litany of events, emotions, and associated feelings was swirling through my head and heart. Striving to heal emotionally became a daily routine. All anyone could talk about for weeks was where they were when the planes hit and how many friends they lost in the WTC collapse. I was talked out; nothing left to say. Nowhere to turn but inward.

How could this event be put into perspective? To many survivors, it either defeated or defined them. The loss of human life and the number of parents, sons, and daughters who died that day were heartbreaking! I could not dismiss this. I could only conclude that moment was meant to startle me in ways I came to understand years later. In retrospect, it changed and defined me. The entirety of the events prompted a torrent of self-discovery and actions that motivated me to become who I am today. It helped me transform in ways I never could have imagined.

After the funeral services were long gone, newspaper headlines countrywide resembled these from New Yorkers affected by the 9/11 events:

> *"Twenty-year Lehman Brothers executive resigns to enroll in a seminary."*
>
> *"Wall Streeter leaves million-dollar trading job to join Teach for America."*
>
> *"Woman executive quits her prestigious banking job to establish a foundation that supports underserved communities."*

Survivors were in pain, soul searching, questioning whether they should stay in the rat race or leave it behind for more fulfilling work. There were many "twists of fate" chronicles of survivors who were supposed to be in the World Trade Center that morning. Many stories were deeply affecting and provoked me to rethink my future. What was the universe communicating? I loved my job and continued to develop skills that led me unpredictably to become a professional speaker, executive coach, and college professor. Who said I had to change careers? Despite the 9/11 stories reported in the media, did it have to be all or nothing? Maybe waiting was the best option. See what happens to my mindset. Assess how I feel at different points along the journey. Timing is important in any job switch, much less a radical transformation.

After serious contemplation, there was no doubt. My career was successful and still evolving. To work under the guidance of Mike Bloomberg was a gift beyond any value I could measure. I had no desire to alter this career...yet. I loved my craft and represented a phenomenal organization. Who would leave that? There was no seminary, vineyard, or more purposeful mission that made sense. Perhaps I was thinking about this all wrong? After a few weeks, I set the career considerations aside. What was troubling me, and how to resolve it? Was I still feeling guilty for being alive? If so, how do I get beyond this?

I eventually worked through this inner turmoil with some unwavering self-talk. "You are no good to your family in a funk. Stop feeling sorry for yourself. Wake up. You're alive! Life is ephemeral." All I could think of was to not let Bill, Peter, and Paul die in vain! What to do?

THE MOUNTAINS WERE CALLING!

Was I losing myself or finding myself? When I started to climb, I didn't know the answer. While alone in my thoughts each day on the commuter train to NYC, the answer came to me in a moment of clarity. The answer to my question can only be answered in action and adventure. I felt the need to get a million miles away from home, office, and career pressures. My inclination was to read a stack of books that might help me feel better. However, I concluded that my goal was not to fill my mind; I had enough of that. Instead, the mission was to clear it. All the mountaineering books described blue skies, endless landscapes, and not many people. That was it! I decided to try it and see where it led me.

On September 11, 2002, I stood on the summit of Mount Rainier in the Cascade Range, sixty miles southeast of Seattle, Washington, as the crow flies. It seemed fitting to climb my first mountain on the one-year anniversary of those heartbreaking World Trade Center events. With an elevation of 14,411 feet above sea level, Rainier is the highest volcanic peak in the contiguous United States. Each year, more than ten thousand people attempt to scale the mountain and use it as a training ground for bigger expeditions. I didn't know where this would lead me, but there was something cathartic about being in this snow-covered alien environment. Something had to change....

By now I stopped asking myself, "Why am I still alive?" I did not want to let my moment of action pass only to regret it later. Something happens to people when confronted with death, setting off a chain reaction that changes people in unexpected ways. Steve Jobs said in his 2005 Stanford University commencement address,

> *"Remembering that you are going to die is the best way I know to avoid the trap of thinking you have something to lose. You are already naked. There is no reason not to follow your heart."*

Climbing a mountain is a mental, physical, and spiritual exercise. I was inspired to follow my heart wherever it led and to let the moment of introspection guide me to do something I had never done. What did I have to lose? I wanted to honor the spirit of my lost friends, to memorialize them uniquely. I had no other thoughts on what, how, or why. I needed to make sense of the signals the world was sending me. There was a force calling, igniting me to explore what mountains lie on the other side of these 9/11 tragedies. Whether by coincidence or fate, the summer before the World Trade Center catastrophe, I read a book by Jon Krakauer called *Into Thin Air*, published in 1997. Although I had not yet climbed a mountain, I was inexplicably drawn to it. *Into Thin Air* recounts a series of tragic events in Nepal on Mount Everest, the world's highest mountain. Krakauer describes incidents on May 10, 1996, when eight climbers died from the convergence and consequences of high altitude, horrific weather, and questionable judgment.

From the opening paragraph, I couldn't put it down. Like most devastating incidents, heroes and villains were identified and caught in a vicious blame game. So many aspects of this story riveted me. And, for better or worse, I began to see myself climbing. The more I learned about mountaineering, the more I envisioned ascending with an ice ax in hand and crampons on both feet. As a distance runner my whole adult life, climbing had many parallels to marathoning. For starters, there was no shortcut to the finish line. Also, besides putting one foot in front of the other, I couldn't control the weather or how others on the same trail would behave.

However, there was one thing under my power: how I chose to act and react to the environment.

No phones or laptops. Also, the stakes were high. This was not just a hobby but a serious pastime. People died climbing mountains. What was I thinking?

Nonetheless, I was intrigued by it all. Mountaineering requires skills, fortitude, and learning to be comfortable in the discomfort of factors beyond anyone's control. One misstep, wrong turn, or slip can lead to catastrophe. Yet, the elation and sense of accomplishment by summiting a peak and reflecting on it later is indescribable. The high is unlike anything I ever felt. Completing a marathon is a remarkable feat but does not compare to stepping on a mountain summit.

I had no expectations and never imagined I would climb so many mountains through the years. I couldn't explain it then. All I could do was accept those feelings and follow where they led. Despite hesitation to leave my family on risky expeditions, something compelled me to see this through. Little did I know that scaling Rainier unleashed a burning desire to climb more and keep finding myself. Mark Twain famously said, "The two most important days in your life are the day you are born and the day you find out why."

On May 16, 2012, descending Alaska's Mount Bona, the highest volcano in the United States, hit me like a proverbial avalanche. Climbing Bona was unlike the six prior alpine expeditions I joined. With three extraordinary guides and eight other climbers, we spent two weeks on a glacier in subzero temperatures, steadily ascending with full packs, hauling equipment up and down the mountain to ensure our safety and survival. We summited on the twelfth day at 16,550 feet above sea level. Using GPS to guide us under the clouds of a blustery snowstorm, we took photos and descended swiftly.

Two days later, settled in at base camp, I reflected on the experience and started to see mountaineering differently. Based on determination, adaptability, and collaboration, mountaineering is a metaphor for how careers are climbed. They had three things in common. Set a goal, take one step at a time, and recognize how critical it is to be part of a team with shared goals.

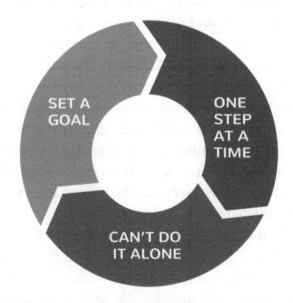

When I thought about my career journey, I was dumbfounded that it took so long to see this. By framing this mountaineering experience to better understand myself, that moment helped me to redefine how I planned to spend the rest of my working life. I thank Mark Twain for helping me discover why I was born.

I began to see myself differently. I recognized the power that mountain guides carry to help transform lives. They are experts in mountaineering and are hired to instruct and lead individuals and small groups. They are also kind, caring, and patient, the qualities used to describe my best teachers. While I had no desire to pursue a career in mountain guiding, they prompted me to soul-search some more.

As I watched how guides led me and my mates, it changed the way I thought about the role of a teacher. My favorites were the sum of instructor, coach, and inspirer. I couldn't help but add therapist, as mountaineering gives new meaning to the word *discomfort*. The guides embolden others who feel reluctant to carry on, shake off their fears, and keep climbing. Those encouraging words speak volumes about a team's capacity to advance, despite low oxygen levels, freezing temperatures, and unpredictable weather. Be it mountains, meeting spaces, or classrooms, I concluded that everyone I meet is on their proverbial mountain, with similar obstacles, challenges, and struggles.

On the flight home from Anchorage to New York, I was prompted by a massive mindset shift. From this day forward, *"I am going to change careers."* I decided to leave the Wall Street world and committed to working each day in the service of someone else's success. If Wall Street was my first career mountain, I was now ready for my second. Mahatma Gandhi's quote was ever-present:

"The best way to find yourself is to lose yourself in the service of others."

In David Brooks' insightful book *The Second Mountain: The Quest for a Moral Life*, he writes, "Our society suffers from a crisis of connection, of solidarity. We live in a culture of hyper-individualism." He explains that many people live somewhere on a continuum. Some move from one extreme to the other, driven by various factors.

SELF   SOCIETY

A LIFE LIVED   A LIFE LIVED
FOR SELF   FOR OTHERS

Brooks states:

> Every so often, you meet people who radiate joy—who seem to know why they were put on this earth, and glow with a kind of inner light. Life, for these people, has often followed what we might think of as a two-mountain shape. They get out of school, start a career, and begin climbing the mountain they thought they were meant to. Goals on this first mountain are the ones our culture endorses: to be a success, to make your mark, to experience personal happiness. But when they get to the top of that mountain, something happens.

They look around and find the view...unsatis-
fying. They realize: This wasn't my mountain
after all. There's another, bigger mountain
out there that is *my* mountain. And so, they
embark on a new journey. On the second
mountain, life moves from self-centered to
other-centered.[1]

Brooks affirms that choosing to climb the second mountain,

is a life of love, care, and commitment. It is an
antidote to much that is wrong with our culture. If the first mountain is about building
up the ego and defining the self, the second
mountain is about shedding the ego and losing the self. You don't climb the second mountain the way you did the first. You conquer
the first but are conquered by the second. You
surrender to some summons and do everything necessary to answer the call. On the first
mountain, you tend to be ambitious, strategic,
and independent. On the second, you are rela-
tional, intimate, and relentless.[2]

Rethinking my life climb as a transition from the first to
the second mountain caused me to make decisions in ways
I could never have foreseen. I came to conclude that one
moment of introspection can lead to actions that become

1   Brooks, David. In *The Second Mountain: The Quest for a Moral Life*, xi. New
     York: Random House, 2020.
2   Ibid.

transformative. I was getting to know myself and came to understand the drive needed to guide others up their proverbial mountains. Brooks so eloquently described how many people move on that continuum, from a life of self to a life lived for others. I am living proof, as are the stories of the wonderful contributors to this book.

As people in my circle shared their stories through the years, I discovered many had moments that sparked life transformations. Each story was unique. However, whether through fate or good fortune, patterns in their narratives began to emerge. The outcomes were distinct, but the lessons were remarkably similar. Certain moments led them to think and act differently. It prompted them to change their entire career.

When I examined what those moments meant to them, we implicitly agreed these became our best teachers and tapped into the deepest sense of our selves. They provoked changes in mindsets and helped us retool for the next proverbial mountain. In all cases these moments were ever lasting and life changing. The lessons gleaned also sparked a massive shift in my education. Unfortunately, I did not have the tools to assist or accelerate the path to knowing myself. I had no insight into how I decided anything and no clue why I did what I did. I operated from experience and intuition but didn't know I could adopt social science tools to help when I needed them most. It was stumble, bumble, and hope for the best. Was there a better way?

Throughout this journey I discovered a social science called Emotional Intelligence (EQ). I was learning to understand and manage my emotions and better able to recognize and influence those around me. I was now empathizing with others in ways that previously seemed foreign. Continuing to absorb and ultimately teach the subject, it started to redefine what it meant to be smart. I was becoming more self-aware; I better understood myself and made more sense of the world around me. I was also asking questions never contemplated. What are my core values? How do I make better decisions? Do people only need tragedy to be a catalyst for personal and/or professional change?

Why had I not learned EQ before? Why was this not taught in school? I began to question the value of my formal education. Nothing I ever memorized for an exam could help me in those moments. Most of my education was spent cramming and taking tests, only to forget most of what I learned one week later. This subject, however, had staying power. Every nugget I learned would not be forgotten. Each proverbial EQ brick could be laid on top of the other, providing a solid foundation by which I discovered the most important subject of all: how to manage myself despite whatever turmoil the world hurled at me.

Consequently, this book is about the moments that define our lives and how to capitalize on them with tools and mental models you never knew existed. With each story of transformation, an Emotional Intelligence tool is explained to illustrate how to measure, monitor, and develop your EQ. To feel what they feel and tie your life circumstances to theirs. I hope you are inspired by the stories you are about to read and encouraged to blaze new trails as you strive to lead a rewarding and fulfilling life.

Thank you for joining me on this journey of self-discovery. Before taking the next big step in the book, I ask you to read aloud and heed this call to action from climbing historian James Ramsey Ullman:

> *"The climbing of earth's heights means little. That men and women want and try to climb them means everything. For it is the ultimate wisdom of the mountains that we are never so much human as when we are striving for what is beyond our grasp, and there is no battle worth the winning save that against our own ignorance and fear."*

Welcome to *The Moment that Defines Your Life*. Be the change you wish to see in the world and climb on!

CHAPTER 1

Develop Your Mental Fortress

In college, many of my classmates studied philosophy. Each evening, when they huddled around the dorm dinner table recounting lessons from well-known ancient Greek thinkers, it sounded so pretentious and lacked any practical orientation. I was lost in the intellectual nature of their debates and too dimwitted to recognize any value in them. I had no idea what they were talking about. Since I was studying finance, how could it possibly help? I dismissed the subject as irrelevant and avoided it like the plague. For the rest of my college days, the mere mention of philosophy made me cringe.

Yet, in my adult life, I began to see glimmers of their discussions wonderfully appear when least expected. Whether a quote from an ancient Greek philosopher or a YouTube video titled "Ten Life Lessons from Friedrich Nietzsche," I started to come around. As I became more curious, most attempts to learn about famous philosophers sadly came from the superficiality of a Wikipedia page. Fortunately, from time to time, I was inspired to take a deeper look into topics that resonated.

More open-minded to the idea that philosophy may have merit, one school spoke to me at unusual times and in surprising places. It also lent credence to the adage, "When the student is ready, the master will appear." It is called Stoicism. And, from my anecdotal and rather unsophisticated conclusion, it is sadly misunderstood.

When I pictured a Stoic, I saw a disheveled man standing in a torrential snowstorm without a hat, coat, or boots. He is staring into a void with a blank expression, devoid of any feeling. Striding through life aimlessly in a continuum of nothingness, one day he dies. To my ignorant teenage mind, that way of life was code for "emotionless." A hollow life with neither passion nor purpose. Now older, and hopefully wiser, I see how Stoicism flips that view upside down. The Stoic chooses how to feel, and subsequently frees their emotions from the control of the external world. As Nassim Taleb, author of the blockbuster book *The Black Swan*, said,

"Stoicism is about the domestication of emotions, not their elimination."

I read about concepts like "frame of mind" and "pushing out of your comfort zone." As I dug deeper into Stoicism's roots, I was calmer and more focused on all matters. My behavior steadily evolved into a powerful means of deciding how to feel when pushing a boulder up a proverbial hill. I no longer felt like the character Sisyphus in Greek mythology. When faced with a struggle, the goal was not to burden my mind with heavy and unproductive thoughts...but to clear it.

Put simply, humans feel first, and think second. If we are taught to think in school, why aren't we taught to feel? Emotions determine your identity, who to befriend, and what you love to do. Anyone in a committed relationship understands the power of emotional appeal, as it can eclipse reason at any time. With the stakes in our lives so high, why leave emotion to chance?

Subsequently, I started to find peace and develop what Rolf Dobelli, a modern-day philosopher refers to in his remarkable book *The Art of the Good Life* as a Mental Fortress. He states, "What can't be taken from you are your thoughts, your mental tools, the way you interpret bad luck, loss, and setbacks. You can call this space your mental fortress—a piece of freedom that can never be assailed." Dobelli is "convinced if we don't have a solid mental toolkit to fall back on, chances are we fail at life. I simply cannot imagine how you could be a successful leader without one." [3] I couldn't agree more.

---

[3]   Dobelli, Rolf. "The Art of the Good Life." In *The Art of the Good Life*, 122–25. New York, NY: Hachette Books, 2017.

Through life's twists and turns, my education did not teach me how to solve problems when things went wrong. If there were coping mechanisms to be learned, I never knew them; I didn't even know where to look. If things were good, no worries. When things went bad, I reacted the only way I knew—mad, sad, upset. All of the above. I could not describe accurately what I felt most of the time. I was not aware of remedies or behavioral modifications to solve problems head-on. I was too much in my head, feeling sorry for myself or in disbelief when facing hardship. I didn't yet understand that people are disturbed not by things but by the view they take of those events.

When I regarded misfortune, like everything that happened on 9/11 and its aftermath, I lacked any depth perception to make sense of it. I oversimplified and deflected all of it as a defense mechanism. By practicing the integration of Stoicism and Emotional Intelligence, I started to develop mental models to deal with the challenges life continually served. I was no longer faltering my way through unforeseen challenges but developing effective tools to overcome them.

I now rely heavily on this philosophy in my executive coaching practice and teach it at Columbia University. Learning to understand Stoicism helped me develop a coping mechanism that was practical and effective. To appreciate this critical puzzle piece, and underscore how it fits thematically into this book, allow me to introduce you to one of the world's greatest leaders, who also happened to be, by all accounts, a wonderful human being.

Marcus Aurelius wrote what some in the publishing community may consider the first "self-help book." He was the last Roman ruler known as the Five Good Emperors, a term coined fourteen centuries later by Niccolò Machiavelli. When you learn about this extraordinary man, living life as a philosopher seemed more important than ruling the world's most powerful empire. He was known to constantly "practice" his philosophy and command the troops without losing his sense of justice and humanity. According to Mark Forstater in *The Spiritual Teachings of Marcus Aurelius*, "The philosophy he lived by is one of empowerment, independence, and self-reliance. Its principles led him to a life of spiritual contentment and worldly attainment, a potent combination that most people still find impossible to achieve."

While busy protecting Roman borders from all sides, he detested war, yet spent many nights in his tent writing a series of thoughts resembling a diary for spiritual development. He wrote about his fears, emotions, and despair at the actions of fellow men and women. He relied on his philosophy to provide the strength needed to adapt to circumstances thrust upon him each day. Aurelius learned to develop his mental fortress in an empire constantly at war and likely found peace in his writings called *Meditations*. Whether intentional or not, he left the world a book on Stoic philosophy that is a bible to me and countless others.

The Romans loved Marcus Aurelius, and he did his best to provide for its citizens through trying times. Growing up, he was a dedicated student and learned Latin and Greek. But his greatest intellectual interest was Stoicism, a philosophy that emphasized fate, reason, and self-restraint. It is based on observations about how the mind and the world work. The Stoics argued that your thoughts and beliefs create the world you inhabit, not external circumstances.

Stoicism teaches us that before we try to control events, start with learning to control ourselves. Our attempts to exert influence on the world are subject to chance, disappointment, and failure, but control of the self is the only kind that can succeed 100 percent of the time.

To see Stoicism in action is a three-pronged approach:

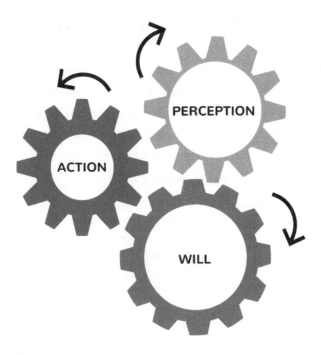

- *Perception:* This requires that we maintain absolute objectivity of thought; that we see things dispassionately for what they are.

- *Action:* The simplest way to understand this is to know that we were made for others, not ourselves. Nature is unselfish and we should be too. We strive to work toward something larger than ourselves, a collective good while treating people justly and fairly.

- *Will:* This encompasses our attitude to things not within our control. Acts of nature such as fire, illness, and even death, however unpleasant, only harm us if we choose to see them that way.

Stoicism has been relied on by some of history's greatest leaders, and practiced by presidents, artists, and entrepreneurs. Football great Tom Brady, singer/songwriter Camila Cabello, and General James Mattis—to name a few—are influenced by Stoic philosophy. To describe them succinctly, a Stoic believes they don't control the world around them, only how they act and react. Add to that, the well-practiced Stoic always responds with the Four Virtues:

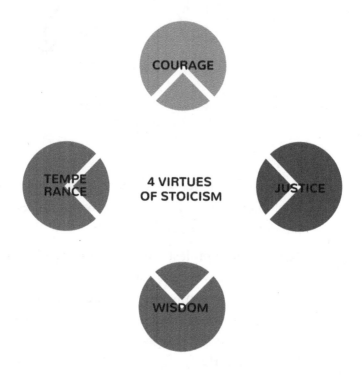

"If, at some point in your life," Aurelius wrote, "should you come across anything better than justice, truth, self-control, or courage—it must be an extraordinary thing indeed."

As a teenager, Marcus believed that in all circumstances, it was necessary to have a set of guidelines one could apply when required to act. As the great Roman Stoic philosopher Seneca said, "Wisdom is harnessing what the philosophy teaches, then wielding it in the real world."

That was two centuries ago. We have discovered many things since then—but have we found anything better than...

...being brave?

...truth and reconciliation?

...doing right by others?

Everything we face is an opportunity to respond with these four traits. Whether during the reign of Roman emperors or living through the COVID crisis, has anything changed regarding the qualities we respect and admire in others? Not likely.

To the Stoic, everything experienced is a matter of judgment. The decisions we make and the opinions we hold are dependent on our state of mind. The ability to decide on events is the only possession within our power, and they believe it is best to be indifferent to things beyond their control. They neither bother nor concern themselves with those matters.

Think about the amount of energy people expend getting caught up in politics, social media, or when cut off in traffic by a random driver. While road rage did not exist two thousand years ago, it is likely people burned enormous amounts of unproductive energy in different ways. What to do when faced with any of these scenarios? The key lies in learning to control the things within our power and subject to our will. If we could bring Marcus into American politics in 2023, I can hear him articulating to a CNN anchor with gusto:

"You always own the option of having no opinion. There is never any need to get worked up or to trouble your soul about things you can't control. These things are not asking to be judged by you. Leave them alone."

As you read this book, your call to action is to develop a Mental Fortress. In other words, what tools are at your disposal to deal with the unpredictable, adversarial, and/or tragic? The good news is that the social science of Emotional Intelligence is the perfect companion to the classic philosophy of Stoicism. It is the ideal blend of what we learned from one of the world's most compassionate leaders two centuries ago, to the evolution of EQ and redefining in the modern era what it means to be smart.

In *Emotional Intelligence: Why It Can Matter More Than IQ,* author Daniel Goleman explained how to keep emotions in check while reading others' innermost feelings and learning to manage those relationships accordingly. Similarly, Marcus Aurelius reflected on the importance of managing emotions by not capitulating to anger and discontent. One learns to calm the mind, a critical aid needed to treat people with civility despite any tension or anxiety between them.

By learning the stories of ordinary people harnessing the power of extraordinary moments, my hope is you begin to see how to convert your moments into astonishing opportunities. Through the integration of Stoicism and Emotional Intelligence:

- Strive to see yourself in these moments.
- Learn to masterfully manage life's ups and downs.

- Take adversity in stride to capitalize on your moments and harness that power into an extraordinary life.

Before you turn the page and discover the wonderful stories written in the service of your transformation, consider Marcus Aurelius' call to action to stop thinking and start doing:

> *"Waste no more time arguing about what a good man should be. Be one."*

CALL TO ACTION

Thoughts, Words, and Actions

Seneca, the great Roman philosopher, encouraged his students to "hunt out the helpful pieces of teaching, and the spirited and noble-minded sayings which are capable of immediate practical application—not far-fetched or archaic expressions or extravagant metaphors and figures of speech—and learn them so well that words become works."

We learn from the Stoics:

- Education is meant to inspire and prompt action.

- Knowledge without action is useless.

- Change is hard.

They also remind us each day there are three things you can control:

- Your attitude.

- Your choices.

- Who you trust.

On any day, as you walk down the street or wait in line for that Starbucks order to be filled, you imagine things to work on such as health, appearance, or career development. Longing to lead a productive life based on actions, too often new ideas ruminating in your mind evaporate into thin air.

Why is it so hard to transform thought into action?
Why do people find it challenging to make positive
and lasting change?

Unfortunately, you may be stalled in patterns that don't serve your desire to change. It is hard and uncomfortable. Fighting it hinders the momentum built over the years to keep yourself safe. But it is in the discomfort where the growth occurs. It is subsequently hard to breach what your mind has been doing for so long. As Warren Buffett often says, "The chains of habit are too light to be felt until they are too heavy to be broken." The heart and mind work hard to protect your status quo.

The contradiction of the human spirit is that we fight to change while we struggle to be the same. We want to change but are often unwilling to pay the price for that pain. The result is a lot of lip service and negative self-talk, attempted shortcuts and dead ends that diminish the spirit. Sadly, when things don't go your way, emotions skyrocket. Thus, the ability to think and act plummets, trapping you in an endless loop, often draining the will to keep trying.

How then to change?

- When faced with a decision point, don't react quickly. Take time to consider your options. Let others wait! Your safety switch activates, dominating the self-talk to do what is safe, not what is in your best interests to change. Blurt your response too quickly, and you may choke on the regrets later. Leo Tolstoy said, "The two most powerful warriors are patience and time." Slow down. What's the rush? Waiting can be an immensely powerful aspect of your decision-making model.

- Give thought to why you want to change. The why becomes your motivation to sustain efforts to keep changing. People begin the change process when they see that the benefit of changing outweighs the discomfort of staying the same. As serial entrepreneur Ryan Blair says often, "If it's important you'll find a way. If not, you'll find an excuse."

- Be the pioneer in your life. In the continuum between protector and pioneer, pioneering comes with risk and is fraught with danger. Where would we be without the pioneers who risked everything and paved the way for us to follow? They were the definitive change agents who accepted the risk inherent in doing what was unknown and uncomfortable.

This is where relying on philosophy comes in. It becomes a part of your self-expression and an inherent part of how you decide anything important. Without a philosophy to guide your work and life, you relentlessly succumb to excuses and distractions. Many make the comfortable mistake of acting on their moods ("I'm just not feeling it today"), not on their principles.

HOW YOU DECIDE:
WHERE IS YOUR CHOICE POINT?

PROTECTOR   PIONEER
COMFORT   DISCOMFORT

In your quest to change, mental barriers are the restraints that keep you where you are. Often, in your quest to change, you struggle to decide how. To assist, whether it is personal development, or you are considering a career change, I developed a mental model to sort through any one of three precepts:

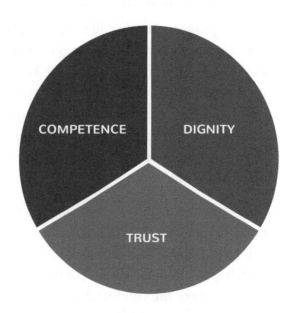

Whatever you decide:

1. Does it serve or expand your circle of competence? Charlie Munger, Warren Buffett's partner, says, "Figure out what your aptitudes are. If you play games where other people have the aptitudes and you don't, you're going to lose. And that's as close to certain as any prediction that you can make. You have to figure out where you've got an edge. And you've got to play within your own circle of competence." The conclusion: If you want to improve your odds of success in life and business, define the perimeter of your circle of competence, and operate inside it.

2. When posed with an opportunity, ask yourself, *"What is not negotiable?"* While I am flexible in many ways, I am inflexible about my values. If a decision tests the limits of my integrity or is associated with something I don't want to be a part of, this model makes it easy to say no. Don't change if it means compromising your circle of dignity. Lean into the change if it is consistent with your values.

3. In the book *Who Not How*, Dan Sullivan poses the question, "What if everything you did was your choice?" When you want to accomplish something, stop asking, "How can I do this?" He teaches his readers instead to ask, "Who can do this for me?" This is your circle of trust. Who can you count on to initiate change? Stoics do not outsource their happiness but are happy to outsource a task to

someone in that circle. Be mindful of who lives there. It can be a lonely place.

"Observe constantly that all things take place by change, and accustom thyself to consider the nature of the Universe loves nothing so much as to change the things which are, and to make new things like them."

Marcus Aurelius

To Misread

*"Unleash in the right time and place before you explode
at the wrong time and place."*
Oli Anderson, author of *Shadow Life*

Verb

1.   Read (a piece of text) wrongly.

2.   Judge or interpret a situation or person's manner
     or behavior incorrectly.

Something was off. Or was I misreading the moment? It was just the two of us in a conference room in Midtown Manhattan. The mission: Prepare my client for the speaking engagement of a lifetime. In eight weeks, several hundred people would pile into an auditorium on Park Avenue and listen to Dan address his company's shareholders. The choreography was set. Wait in the wings, listen to the introduction, walk toward the lip of the stage...stand and deliver! Given the high stakes of this event, in the words of Gene Kranz, an American aerospace engineer featured in the movie *Apollo 13*, "Failure is not an option."

With a CPA, MBA, and Ivy League pedigree, Dan's name usually surfaced when describing "the smartest person in the room." He was the chief financial officer of a large New York City–based investment management firm and a wealth of knowledge on all matters of finance. He dreamed in time that one day he would become this company's chief executive officer (CEO). Before we met, I was told by a friend who worked with him in another company, "When things were going well, he's confident, collaborative, and funny. He can also be polite and respectful...until he isn't." While I did not initially understand the implication of his comments, it later became clear as day.

I was subsequently hired by the company's actual CEO to coach Dan through the "speech of his career." He expressed no doubt about Dan's coachability, certain he would work diligently to deliver an exceptional presentation. But lately he witnessed "something different" in Dan's temperament and struggled to understand why, after fourteen years of steadfast dependability, he "seemed to have changed." The CEO couldn't put his finger on it. With no evidence offered, he simply communicated how important it was to help Dan in this step of his evolution. As our meeting ended, he slipped in rather effortlessly, "Let me know what you discover about his behavioral changes. I am concerned for him and my firm." As I left the meeting, those words rang endlessly through my head. His message was loud and clear.

Before any executive coaching project, I am mindful of a universal premise that people want to be understood and accepted. Listening is the most effective method we can make to get there. Since I did not know Dan, all I had heading into this assignment were the thought-provoking observations of two individuals I respected. By getting acquainted over lunch, my goal was to remove any biases and show a sincere desire to understand how best to be of service.

It was critical to earn his trust and underscore that I was there to help him develop into a clear, concise, and compelling communicator. There was one goal at the onset: maximize Dan's effectiveness on that stage. Nothing else mattered. However, there are always proverbial landmines and other unpredictable factors that can derail any well-planned mission. Nevertheless, what I learned from Chris Voss' powerful book *Never Split the Difference* about human beings is, "We are crazy, irrational, impulsive emotional driven animals." All the raw intelligence and logic does little to shift the interplay of two people collaborating. Consequently, three questions always swirl in my mind on high-stakes coaching engagements: How well will we bond? How effectively will he learn my techniques? What does the path ahead look like? My mindset was to take this one step at a time and see where the mountain would lead us.

Before our first meeting, notwithstanding any additional input, I drafted a three-pronged professional development plan:

- **External Dan:** Teach him communication skills that inspire, persuade, and provoke change from my book *A Climb to the Top*.

- **Internal Dan:** Understand Dan's natural tendencies and help him develop tools to stay calm under the weight of great expectations.

- **Measure Progress:** Monitor and coach as needed the integration of the two points above.

When we met, Dan was the bastion of professionalism. However, there were a few days during training when I sensed behavioral foibles hinted at by his CEO. The cues were subtle. Without a heads-up, they would not prompt anyone to notice. I chalked one observation up to Dan just having a bad day. Although I couldn't predict when, he occasionally came to meetings distracted, lacking the focus I was accustomed to seeing on his more productive days. Which Dan would show on any given coaching session? Calm and cool? Or anxious and ill-tempered? Each meeting was a coin toss.

At first, I shrugged off the inconsistencies. Usually, when he practiced communications techniques, he was attentive and worked diligently to master the Ten Commandments of Great Communicators from my book *A Climb to the Top*. On other days, I had trouble making sense of his uneven behavior. I often dismissed it, thinking this would eventually resolve itself. It is not unusual when training executives under pressure to observe less than flattering behavior. The tension turns out to be positive, productive, and where most of the learning occurs. The mentee eventually self-corrects, stays focused on the mission, and reverts to his/her typical self. Up to this point, I had not yet seen the full extent of the Dan described by his CEO. Will that Dan emerge? Were the CEO's instincts wrong?

Then, on our fourth meeting, out of the clear blue sky, it happened! Dan and I gathered at a table to discuss some critical points he needed to include in his presentation. In attendance were three of his colleagues and a woman named Linda, a strategic consultant hired to assist in the firm's growth strategy. Fifteen minutes into the meeting, Linda asked Dan a seemingly innocuous question. With no fore-thought or pause, he stood up, looked into her eyes, and let loose a tirade. It was a verbal explosion unlike any I had seen or heard in my coaching business. He pushed back from the table with a force none of us were expecting. He looked down at Linda, directly into her eyes, with index finger drawn, he symbolically pushed the words of his explosive tirade at her. Taken off guard by Dan's shameless behavior, she pulled back in her chair, prepared to defend herself as if in a bar room brawl. Yet, when he was done, he took no time to spread his discontent further, ignoring Linda and storming down the hall, babbling how he was surrounded by idiots. He was a frenzy of malice who exploded in a way I had not seen or heard in my coaching business. Here's a sample:

> *"What do you know? You sit in meetings all day, nodding your head, talking nonsense. Are you incompetent or just stupid?"*

Offensive and condescending, it was a gruesome moment for Linda to be on the receiving end of this volcanic eruption. Two professionals locked in conflict, precipitated by a question seeking clarity on a routine matter.

WHAT DID I JUST OBSERVE, INTERNALIZE, AND CONCLUDE?

First, a mismatch between meeting expectations and what occurred. Second, a woman on the receiving end of a pro-verbial assault who felt threatened, first by words, then by actions. Third, a moment with a seasoned veteran whose reputation was shattered in a split second. Twenty years to climb the career mountain. A moment to fall off the proverbial cliff.

What happened and why? Dan had an emotional meltdown witnessed by colleagues that had a ripple effect across his organization. In a moment, doubts were flying through the firm. In conference rooms throughout the company, questions abounded:

- "What caused such an outburst?"
- "Is he fit for the C-suite?" (That's a reference to a company's executive-level managers.)
- "Can he ever be considered for CEO with such a short fuse?"

In a meeting the next day, their chief operating officer (COO) was overheard saying, "This has been bubbling for a long time. He seemed so off his game these past few months. We should have seen it coming."

The moment arrived! While the firm was alarmed by Dan's erratic behavior, it paled in comparison to their apprehension of the reputational risk of a leader's appalling and inexcusable conduct. In the words of Daniel Goleman in his book *Emotional Intelligence: Why It Can Matter More than IQ*, he states,

> *"CEOs are hired for their intellect and business expertise, and fired for their lack of emotional intelligence."*

The moment I experienced with Dan was a watershed event for him. It may not have been a dismissible moment, but it diminished his capacity for consideration for CEO. It took a split second to determine what went wrong. It also became a turning point, the moment that helped Dan conclude the most critical aspect of his job. It had little to do with his competence or Ivy League education. Plenty of people look just as good on a resume. That seminal moment became his best teacher. He recognized it in hindsight, which caused him to redefine what it meant to be smart. Stepping on that stage in a few weeks suddenly took a back seat to mend the damage done to his reputation.

Dan recognized the impact of his actions, and in turn the need to apologize to Linda. He wanted not only to save his reputation but to mend the bonds that were broken that day. Furthermore, he felt the need to apologize to everyone who had been on the receiving end of his abysmal behavior these last few months. He realized it was the only path to erase the baggage associated with his prior actions. He showed vulnerability and humility by asking the same people he offended for help.

This scenario plays out across offices and work environments every day across the globe. Unfortunately, it is all too common. Many people chalk it up to, "That's business." Be aggressive. Don't show weakness. This isn't personal; it's business. Dismiss anything but results as irrelevant or inconsequential. Who knew?

Watching Dan erupt like that hit me like a lightning bolt! It was early in my Climb Leadership business. I was hired to coach executives and teach them what I did for years at Bloomberg. Step on stage, deliver a speech, and persuade the audience to buy all things Bloomberg. If they left with memorable insights and a strong call to action, mission accomplished. If not, it was a waste of their time and my failure.

When I started teaching these skills, I hadn't realized that most people I was working with were a jumble of fears. They showed massive anxiety when called on to speak publicly. Immediately, I saw emotional reactions I had not witnessed before. As they were learning communication tactics, including "Pause Power" and "Speak in the Rule of 3" from my Ten Commandments framework, their temperament and composure were on display and often uncontrollable.

Besides fearful, they were often exhausted, tied up in knots at the prospect of what they were expected to do so far out of their comfort zones. I soon discovered that the fear is manifested in something known as Emotional Hijacking. Right in front of me, intelligent, well-educated people were asked to do something seemingly simple. Get in front of others and tell them what you want them to know, think, and/or feel. For some seasoned professionals, these opportunities require little or no preparation. They practice their craft all day, every day. How hard could it be to communicate to others the expertise they work so diligently to acquire? For others, this is a colossal mountain filled with challenges and pitfalls unlike anything they ever experienced.

I subsequently concluded in a moment of astonishing clarity that I needed to change or augment my teaching methods. These moments forced me to examine what

I was missing and determine how to be a better teacher and coach. I finally realized I was not training people to communicate...yet.

Instead, by helping them confront their fears and developing a plan to move past them, they were transforming into something bigger and better.

Clients were learning my communication techniques but were often disconnected from any emotional responses causing them to operate so poorly in front of others. They said the right words, but their approach was either devoid of any feeling or overwhelmed by anxiety. Their tone was lifeless. There was no passion, as they were solely aiming not to make any mistakes, which is hardly a formula to inspire and persuade. The key was figuring out how to help them seize control of their emotions and use these moments as building blocks for personal and professional change.

It was clear that the key to optimal performance when public speaking went far beyond the tools described in *A Climb to the Top*. I discovered that the companion to compelling communication skills is helping people wrest control of their emotions. I subsequently developed techniques for emotional intelligence development, juxtaposed with public speaking skills to help executives transform into astonishing communicators. Add to that a newfound interest in Stoicism, and I was beginning to see people differently and found many ways to help them significantly discover and advance their internal and external selves.

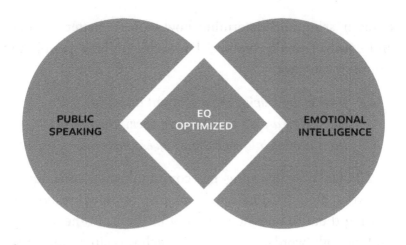

The insight gleaned from that moment with Dan under-scored a key tenet of career ascension. Career climbers can grow boundlessly or stall endlessly. Dan, like so many professionals, was promoted on the strength of his technical competence. He performed admirably in school as he crammed and memorized his way to academic success. Having chosen a profession that requires an abundance of technical skills, what happens when that circle of competence expands beyond your comfort zone and becomes a catalyst for questionable behavior? What does one say to their boss when asked to communicate in a meeting, on camera, or, more terrifying, in front of a large audience? Despite the pressure, these moments have massive implications on how people act, react, and respond to each other. At first, I was hyper focused on my client's outside...how they present. What I realized with increasing frequency, to get that right, the development starts elsewhere. I will forever be grateful for such a simple yet profound discovery.

In a world of highly educated, intelligent, hardworking people, technical competence is rarely questioned. Behavior, however, is a different matter. In a stressful moment, when interacting with others, who do you turn to for assistance? You choose what to say and how to say it and wait for the listener to respond. There is no one there to coach or correct you in the event of a misstep. Every word and gesture can be an intentional act of positivity and goodwill. Or, it can be an embarrassing, incoherent collection of words and phrases, leaving the listener to wonder about your mental state. You were not taught nor conditioned on how to react in the heat of inflammatory discussions or when faced with a challenging interpersonal hurdle. Your formal education taught you to learn by rote, not how to behave in unpredictable moments and/or adverse situations.

On the outside, Dan strived to maintain his composure. If he was an iceberg, you saw the tip. Competent, professional, courteous. Below the surface, quite the opposite. Dan felt handcuffed by his fears and too afraid to reveal them. Vulnerability was a weakness as he grew up in the school of "Never let them see you sweat."

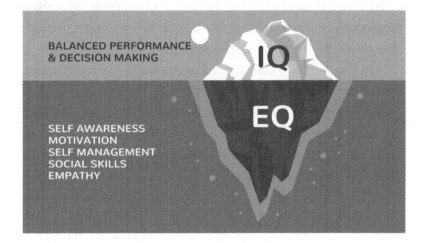

Inside, Dan was a nervous wreck, proverbially scared to death. Mentally exhausted. He put up quite a front every day! Far out of his competency, he feared what would happen if he stepped on stage and botched his presentation. What would be the consequences given the visibility of this event?

His tough exterior masked a bundle of nerves that, if not controlled, could hijack the senses and prompt emotional dysfunction at the most inopportune time. He exhibited what I see in executives all the time. Called Imposter Syndrome, he was constantly questioning himself. "How am I supposed to step on a stage in front of all these people without puking? When will I be discovered as a fraud? I was trained to be an accountant. All that education for what? How am I supposed to do this?"

Prior to our coaching project, in every instance of public speaking, Dan felt unprepared and ill-equipped. Nevertheless, he understood in companies worldwide, the top jobs go to the most compelling communicators. In his quest to be the next CEO, he recognized it would not happen by accident or by default. Dan also concluded that to earn that spot, the characteristics that propelled him to CFO were not the same traits leading to the chief executive summit. Called the Paradox of Success explained by Marshall Goldsmith in his book *What Got You Here Won't Get You There*, Dan finally understood how important the book's title is for anyone's career climb.

Many in his organization took for granted that his intellect and work ethic were all he needed to deliver a powerful and compelling presentation. People assumed he "would figure it out" and "deliver to the same exacting professional standards" expected when he met with colleagues and clients. Yet in recognizing this, I was prompted to draw another conclusion I needed to address: The behavioral traits on display at the office are the same as seen when with family and friends. When I speak to the spouses of the people I coach, it is clear the behavioral tendencies are the same. Fear and loathing in the office bring fear and loathing home. Can these EQ traits be improved in both professional and personal lives? Is there any difference between the two?

For better or worse, it's all personal. With the advent of the internet, there is hardly a clear line of demarcation between work and home. We are always on, constantly communicating, with barely a relief valve. It is taxing enough to work under pressure, keep a marriage healthy, and raise well-adjusted children. Who teaches you to adapt and stay calm under the weight of pressure coming at you from every career and life corner?

When I considered my project with Dan, the mission was not just to train him to communicate with power and precision. I mistakenly put the proverbial cart before the horse. Who knew that beneath it all, I was helping Dan to do something more foundational? If we didn't address the emotional dimension of his intelligence, Dan would be doomed to fail. I learned that to polish the outside, begin from the inside.

As we came to know each other more intimately (typical in one-on-one coaching assignments), in a moment of emotional candor, he explained how his life had unraveled these past few years. It was no coincidence he was coming to work angry, unable to control his emotions, and making others feel small. He tried hard to hide it but eventually blew up. He brought proverbial baggage to work each day, unable to muster the strength to think beyond the destruction within himself to see the impact he had on his colleagues.

In the process of a highly contentious divorce and estranged from his two children, he never shared nor let on to anyone at work the struggles he was working through. Like a good soldier, he went to work armed with technical competence but lacked an emotional fortress (more on that in subsequent chapters) that kept him constantly off balance, leaving him vulnerable and constantly on guard.

That moment with Linda was his perfect storm. Every aspect of his life collided at that moment. It was a great opportunity to reflect on his behavior, explain the foundations of Emotional Intelligence, and help him go to/from work each day equipped with an expanded tool kit.

However, given his responsibility to step on that stage in a few weeks and deliver a powerful and compelling speech, no one cared what Dan's life was like away from the office. His fear of public speaking, the state of his crumbling marriage, or how he scored on an Emotional Intelligence assessment was of no relevance to anyone. However, that's where we adjusted the coaching plan...by measuring and developing his Emotional Intelligence.

A TIME TO MEASURE, A TIME TO MONITOR, A TIME TO GROW

I discussed with Dan that EQ has a foundation comprised of four parts—Self-Awareness, Self-Management, Social Awareness, and Relationship Management. Since Wall Street executives respond better to performance indicators than anecdotes, experience prompted me to take a logical, analytical approach to a development plan rooted as much in emotion as in logic. Until he saw metrics to validate these EQ conclusions, there was little I could do to convince him how much he needed this. It was my responsibility to demonstrate the evidence, relevance, and consequence of inaction. If he didn't see the proof, he would never accept the help he so badly needed. Before demonstrating Dan's score, it was critical he understood what the assessment means and why it matters. Hence, I started by defining each EQ dimension and followed them up with his scores:

Self-Awareness: The ability to focus on yourself and how your actions, thoughts, or emotions do or don't align with your internal standards.

Self-Management: The ability to regulate one's emotions, thoughts, and behaviors effectively in different situations.

Social Awareness: The ability to take the perspective of and empathize with others, including those from diverse backgrounds and cultures.

Relationship Management: A person's process of managing and optimizing interactions with his/her friends, families, and colleagues.

Dan's EQ Profile	
Personal Competence	71
Self-Awareness	69
Self-Management	71
Social Awareness	77
Relationship Management	67

Dan's EQ assessment showed he was low on Self-Awareness and Relationship Management relative to the other two pillars. I pointed out where he was on the scale—the evidence. I then showed anecdotal verification from a 360-degree peer review, a development tool to provide feedback from colleagues in his organization. I met ten of his co-workers, from a CEO to a recently hired college graduate who worked with him. They described similar behavioral patterns. For Dan to see those comments on paper became a startling revelation. The EQ assessment integrated with his peer review was a seminal moment! And in his words, "A gift."

He lacked the Self-Awareness to understand what was happening in front of him. Regrettably, he sacrificed relationships that took him twenty years to build, only to watch his credibility erode in a few short months. Yet, Dan did not let the burden of this knowledge crush him. His tenacity had seen him through this far into his career and drove him through the change he needed to make within himself. He did not become technically competent by submitting to failure, and fortunately recognized the same could be said for Emotional Intelligence. He acknowledged the challenges that together we were committed to resolving.

For starters, it was important to outline and explain the tools necessary to become more emotionally intelligent. Deep down inside he was a good-hearted and generous individual. But he did not know how to deal with his unhappiness without lashing out at anyone in his vicinity. He never learned a coping mechanism to control his unpredictable outbursts and was not sufficiently self-aware to note that change was needed. He lacked the tools to temper the anger and failed to adjust his behavior when he felt bouts of rage emerging. Most people understand these instances and admit they have behaved in ways they later regretted. Remaining calm under the weight of pressure and competing interests can cause the most easygoing personality to become emotionally hijacked at inopportune moments. It made Linda feel so bad that, six years later she recounts that episode with stunning clarity.

To succeed these days requires a key ingredient that is as important as the air we breathe...and it's called Emotional Intelligence (EQ). Emotional Intelligence is not a formal subject in the conventional education system. For many it is developed individually, through trial and error throughout their lifetimes. Yet, in the twenty-first century, it is a skill many companies demand from their employees. No matter your major, did you take courses in college to help you redefine what it means to be smart? Not likely! When you consider the LinkedIn top five soft skills sought by employers in this era, note how Emotional Intelligence made the grade.

TOP SOFT SKILLS

CREATIVITY
PERSUASION
COLLABORATION
ADAPTABILITY
EMOTIONAL INTELLIGENCE

Consequently, the rest of this book explains why being emotionally intelligent and learning about Stoicism redefines what it means to be smart and accelerates career climbs. It provides tools to learn and practice that have enormous career and life implications. While there are many books on these subjects, my goal is to cut through the confusion and provide the clarity needed to attain the right balance of EQ, Stoicism, and cognitive psychology. I have trained thousands of people at companies like JP Morgan Chase and Johnson & Johnson and teach this subject at Columbia University.

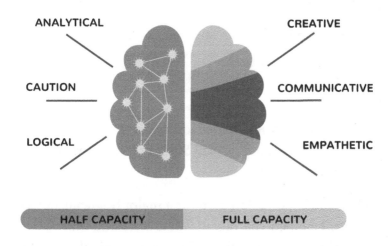

Still, so many are unaware of its power and importance. Rather, your temperament, effective communication, and, most important, maintaining composure under the weight of enormous pressure are competencies you can develop. Becoming emotionally intelligent does not happen by accident. It is no different than learning math, English, music, or any other subject. In this book, you will read stories of ordinary people confronted with extraordinary moments that changed lives, careers, and/or both. In each are lessons and prescriptions for how best to work through those transformative moments.

There are a variety of tools we use in our everyday activities that involve empathy, social awareness, and relationships. In addition, there is an entire side of the brain we barely develop. Listen to advice from Jamie Dimon, CEO of JP Morgan Chase, one of the world's most successful financial institutions. He communicates the three characteristics he seeks when hiring:

- Capability,
- Character, and
- How you treat others.

Nowhere in my formal education did anyone mention the path to Wall Street in the context of Dimon's frame.

On a CEO succession plan for a major financial services company, I helped the organization conclude that the top three attributes they sought in the next individual to take the company helm were:

- Grace under fire,
- Resolves conflict effectively, and
- Empathetic leadership style.

This organization did not care who had the highest grades, SAT scores, or what college they attended. Leaders who had strong pedigrees but lacked Emotional Intelligence were quickly ruled out of the CEO selection process. When you see these commonalities, is it any wonder that Emotional Intelligence is seen and respected as a critical leadership competency?

My students at Columbia University's Graduate School of Engineering are prime examples of the need to develop hard and soft skills simultaneously. I teach in a program called PDL, short for Professional Development and Leadership. Driven by employer demand for greater soft skills in their engineers, the program was designed in response to company frustrations that the leadership and communication skills of our graduates needed to significantly improve. In other words, how best to augment the education of a profession that stresses technical competence and often dismisses these skills as irrelevant. To succeed beyond their engineering domains, the companies wanted their engineers to learn communication skills and emotional intelligence as cornerstones of their education.

"Work with people from the inside out" became my teaching approach. Don't even teach Pause Power or the Rule of 3 from *A Climb to the Top* until the inside, the invisible side, is equipped. Anyone can step on a stage and speak with power. But very few can do so without addressing what emerges on the inside. Like a volcano, the lava building up is an apt metaphor for people who work under pressure. When will that eruption occur? How much damage will be inflicted by the time that outburst is complete? As Warren Buffett said in Rolf Doblli's *The Art of the Good Life*, "I am not very good at solving problems. I am good at avoiding them." His mantra is a call to action that learning to be emotionally intelligent is a critical competency to avoid the interpersonal struggles that come with everyday human interactions.

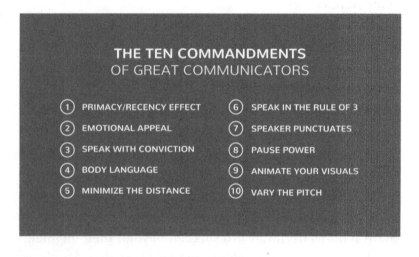

THE TEN COMMANDMENTS
OF GREAT COMMUNICATORS

1. PRIMACY/RECENCY EFFECT
2. EMOTIONAL APPEAL
3. SPEAK WITH CONVICTION
4. BODY LANGUAGE
5. MINIMIZE THE DISTANCE
6. SPEAK IN THE RULE OF 3
7. SPEAKER PUNCTUATES
8. PAUSE POWER
9. ANIMATE YOUR VISUALS
10. VARY THE PITCH

It took a moment for Dan to recognize three things that became life-changing:

- He finally admitted to himself that he was under enormous pressure at work and home, causing distractions and outbursts toward the people he cared most about. The conversations he had with himself were a web of evasion and self-deception. Since it was so painful to admit to himself the truth, just getting to be numb each day without any EQ prescription was good enough.

- He was afraid to share his pain, thinking he could solve his own emotional challenges. He bottled his anxiety deep inside, until enough pressure blew the lid off.

- He never developed a coping mechanism. Dan was emotionally exhausted by the amount of energy expended, striving to control his behavior in stressful situations. He kept his fears under the covers, not wanting to reveal anything that could be perceived as unstable. He was not mentally tough. Unconditioned to confront his shortcomings, it took one instant of emotional dysfunction to realize the consequences of his actions. At that moment, the world spoke to him. He came to conclude from others who he was. And he was appalled and embarrassed at what he saw in the mirror.

TIME FOR CHANGE

My biggest revelation through years of coaching executives is that specific moments in our lives, for better or worse, become our best teachers. They are often sudden, intuitive moments of clarity initiated by something simple and usually painful. What to do with these moments? What do you learn about yourself? How to turn negative moments into constructive outcomes and positive moments into astonishing success?

Consequently, moments like what happened to Dan become indelibly marked in a person's psyche for a lifetime.

For better or worse, these moments happen at unpredictable times and in unexpected places. What to do with your best and worst moments and turn them into the finest education you never paid for?

More importantly, what happens when that moment involves the love of your life?

CALL TO ACTION

To Misread

"*The nearer a man comes to a calm mind, the closer he is to strength.*"

Marcus Aurelius

According to a 2010 study published in the *Journal of Medicine and Life*, there is a positive correlation between "negative emotions and conditions such as...coronary heart disease." The same study found connections between anger and diabetes. Sadly, people struggle with anger daily. You see it everywhere because it is a natural human reaction. The Stoics help us question those angry responses and develop behavior to overcome it. No matter the gender, marital status, or profession, the inability to control anger with people in your life is costly.

Though symptoms vary, anger issues come in many forms, including...

- Feeling constantly overwhelmed,
- Consistently "ranting" or "blowing up," and
- Becoming easily involved in arguments.

THE MOMENT THAT DEFINES YOUR LIFE

> *"Anger and the sorrow it produces are far more harmful than the things which make us angry."*
>
> Marcus Aurelius

I unfortunately meet many people who become like the individuals they constantly decry. It is evident on television and radio every night in our highly contested political climate. Sadly, humans tend to become their own worst enemies and behave like the people they despise. Marcus often communicates in *Meditations* there is no merit in behaving that way. You show moral character when you take the high ground and resist the impulse to heave anger at others.

> When it takes over, all inner peace vanishes. It is tempting to punish others who offend or put us down. However, you continue to perpetuate that circle of hatred and ignorance. It is time to start practicing the EQ tool of empathy and put yourself in their shoes. They may be going through a rough patch, have been diagnosed with an illness, or are just having a bad day. As US President Barack Obama said, "The biggest deficit that we have in our society and in the world right now is an empathy deficit. We are in great need of people being able to stand in somebody else's shoes and see the world through their eyes."

Next time you are in a heated argument or feel anger bubbling up suddenly, try these coping techniques:

1. Stop talking. Start counting, 1...2...3. If you still feel like you are going to erupt, keep counting, 4...5...6. The silence will feel awkward. Let it! By staying silent, at least for several seconds, you will not regret what you never said. Note how good it feels to suppress the anger in the heat of that moment and show through body language your attempt to stay calm despite the stress.

2. As you count, put yourself in their shoes. It can be rough! They made you angry. Why give them that consideration? They gained the upper hand and made you feel small. In a no-win situation, sometimes it is best to settle for the least-worst alternative. Say nothing and walk away. Let cool heads prevail. In the interim, if you feel they have belittled you, consider what Epictetus said: "If you want to improve, be content to be thought foolish and stupid."

"We will ensure that we do not become angry if we put before our eyes all the vices anger gives rise to and take good measure of them. We must accuse and condemn anger, scrutinize its crimes and expose it to the light of day, compare it with the worst evils so that we can see clearly what it is."
Seneca

CHAPTER 3

Bob Litwin: To Serve

"I felt like all the training was for this. It is for the match I am in now, this match of Carol's illness. And as much as I wanted to be a successful competitor in tennis, I wanted to be a total winner in dealing with her sickness whichever way it was going."

Verb

1. Perform duties or services for another person or an organization.

2. Present food or drink to someone.

Noun

3. (In tennis and other racquet sports) An act of hitting the ball to start play.

B ob Litwin recognizes that peoples' beliefs, attitudes, and thoughts cause them to underperform in pursuit of their goals—and developed a solution to solve that problem. He is the founder of the Focus Coaching Group, LLC, and provides coaching programs for companies and individuals in every business sector and sport. With over four decades of coaching top athletes, Wall Street traders, and analysts to raise performance to extraordinary levels, he is a master of change, both for himself and others. His approach is based on a proprietary method called The New Story.

His astounding methodology is documented in *Live the Best Story of Your Life: A World Champion's Guide to Lasting Change*, a remarkable book that had a colossal impact on me. Powerful and compelling, it is one of two books (the other is Dale Carnegie's *How to Win Friends and Influence People*), I recommend to all my clients and students. I read it many times, synthesized each chapter in a Word document, and keep it handy in my briefcase. Whether on a plane, subway, or sipping coffee at Starbucks, I read chapter summaries often and feel his masterful influence. It harnesses the power of your story and provides a guide to creating positive shifts in any area of your life. His methods do not shift what you do but who you are.

As if that isn't enough, Bob is a tennis champion, a number one world-ranked senior tennis player, and a twenty-seven-time US National Champion. As he started playing tennis tournaments seriously at age thirty-two, his early frustrations in competition led him to develop The Focused Game Method, a system to find and sustain maximum focus. He often won at all levels in practice when there was nothing on the line. Yet when it mattered, he lost to players he perceived were less skilled. Bob subsequently concluded that the solution was to significantly improve his capacity to concentrate under pressure. While talent and ability are important to play, the critical aspect was altering his mindset to optimize performance and consistently win. His methods transcend tennis and apply to every aspect of life. Enjoying astonishing success into his mid-seventies, this is but one stage of his story. There is another period that changed his life. At first blush, it does not appear to have anything to do with tennis or coaching. On further examination, it has everything to do with both.

In the spring of 2010, Bob watched Carol, his soulmate of twenty-eight years, lose her three-year battle with cancer. His defining moment was after Carol's breast cancer diagnosis. Although the initial shock was devastating, he grounded himself in the realization that, although terrible, it was nonetheless treatable. While this diminished his worries, the realization of life's fragility was at the forefront of his mind. However, the bad news continued to evolve as medical treatment proved to be veering in the wrong direction.

Bob accepted that the diagnosis was life-threatening and could kill his beloved wife. He realized that all his tennis training—mental, physical, emotional, and spiritual—culminated in this moment. As much as he wanted to be a successful tennis competitor, he was now playing for enormous stakes far beyond the outcome of any tennis match. He wanted to be a winner in dealing with her illness. While he was accustomed to serving tennis balls on the court, more important was how he chose to serve Carol. Although she eventually passed away, his new story was beginning to emerge.

Two months later, the hip surgery he had several months earlier had failed. He was the number one senior tennis player in the world and could scarcely take a step without medical intervention. While he was distraught at losing Carol, he also felt hopeless, as he could neither walk nor play the game he so adored.

FOR THE FIRST TIME IN HIS LIFE, BOB WANTED TO GIVE UP

Yet, not long after her passing, while looking in the mirror, he heard Carol's voice tenderly say, "What would you tell a client?" In his next defining instance, he needed a new story. "It was that moment when I realized I want to be the best version of myself. I want to be the best Bob I could ever be." But how?

While reflecting on the circumstances, he sat down at his computer and wrote a new story. Not a story of where he was. He had enough of that. But a new one of where he wanted to be in his life. A better story. A story of optimism. A story of hope. Relying on the Japanese concept of Kaizen, he sought a story he could move toward one step at a time. He realized, "Change happens less when people make huge commitments." Instead, his mindset shift was, "Don't underestimate the power of small steps, and celebrate those milestones along the way." His new story started with:

> *"I am young. I am strong. I am not alone. I have friends and family who will be with me. I have the inspirational memory of Carol pushing through chemo and radiation. I have gone through surgery and rehab once, and I can do it again. I am a master of rehab. The surgery will be a step to full health. My middle name is resilience, and I will*

be back on the tennis court within three months.
I will be competing again. I love the challenge of
dealing with adversity. I am a model for those
around me in pushing through difficult experi-
ences. I will grow from this experience. I am over-
flowing with life. I am a vessel of love. I have had
one angel in my life. I will find another."

What ultimately became a template for his clients to write their new stories, he suddenly came alive. Within days he scheduled a hip replacement, made hospital and post-operative arrangements, and was excited at what the future would bring. It was time to move from his old story toward the new one. With the surgery a success, within a year he was back on the court accelerating into the most exciting chapter of his life. Business was booming; he was a finalist in a national championship and was inducted into the Eastern Tennis Hall of Fame, an organization that honors significant contributors on and off the tennis court. And the best part... he found another angel. He was now writing his new story and living it. As stated in his magnificent book,

> *"You are about to get a gift...this is going to come in*
> *the form of a special skill."*

In *Live the Best Story of Your Life*, Bob references Amanda Ripley's book *The Unthinkable: Who Survives When Disaster Strikes—and Why*. "Since half of all Americans have been affected by a disaster, she brings light into civilization's darkest moments and poses some daunting questions. Why do we freeze in the middle of a fire? Why does our sight and hearing change during a terrorist attack? She discusses the science of how human fear short circuits work, why our instincts misfire, and how we can change that." Ripley's lesson: "Change before you must. Ergo the flood comes, and you have no ark. Anticipate. Prepare. Train. You never know when the next flood is coming."

Bob's conclusion: "We are all masters of denial." His tools became a training ground for anyone working through struggles and adversity. "When things are going well, we tend to be complacent about training our attitude and spirit...but that is the time to keep practicing. You are always training for the unthinkable."

Several years later, Bob reflects on that period of his life as not the happiest...but the best. "With the most texture: love, devotion, caring for Carol and others. Family, freedom from self-judgement, living in the present, and personal growth." All the training that he stumbled into prepared Bob for any of life's colossal challenges. His call to action for the lives he touches and the communities he has built is:

> *"Train now before tragedy hits so you can deal with your life like a champion."*

WHAT BOB LEARNED IN THOSE MOMENTS

Bob solidified his core values and learned that being the best version of himself did not have to be a selfish act. He made a clear distinction that the "best time" was not "the happiest." That's an important lesson that sustaining personal growth can occur in the saddest of tragedies. It was critical to have this perspective to optimize his contribution to everyone in his orbit, from clients to caring for Carol in her last days. He also learned to shift his focus to work on ways of "being," not simply of "speaking."

Although I have never seen or heard Bob reference the philosophy of Stoicism, I suspect if he met Marcus Aurelius, they would have a lot to talk about. When I consider what Bob has taught me, it starts by recognizing three principles:

- The story we have all been sold on change...has changed.

- Small changes matter.

- Once you see change as a story you tell yourself, the world opens to endless possibilities.

All this begins with accepting where you are in life (your old story) and deciding where you want to take it (your new story). When you start to notice your change, the critic's voice arrives, telling you all the reasons why it won't work. But, from Bob's point of view, once you make up your mind, "This is your life. You get to make the rules. What do you have to lose?"

INTEGRATING BOB'S STOICISM AND EMOTIONAL INTELLIGENCE

In Stoicism, acceptance does not come from a place of surrender but from a place of strength. Stoics refer to accepting what you cannot control and moving on as the art of acquiescence. Stoicism is about accepting what lies outside your locus of control. Unfortunately, minds are prone to agonizing over the future or the past, spending hours ruminating over completely fictional events. To Bob's point, "You don't have to have an adversarial relationship with change anymore." Acceptance is coming to terms with what is real, including Carol's illness and Bob's potentially career-ending hip injury.

It has nothing to do with whether you're happy and everything to do with a peaceful acknowledgment of the concrete things in your life that are true. The path toward acceptance (and your new story) asks two questions:

- Can this be changed?
- If not, what needs to be done to accept this—mentally, physically, emotionally—so you can move on to your new story?

Acceptance yields freedom. When your emotions are no longer at the mercy of external events, you are free to expend energy on efforts that are productive and fulfilling.

Bob realized that in the process of transforming himself, he had to accept that he could not predict the outcome. This did not scare him, as he needed to work on his new story and accept with blind faith that it would take hold and change him. This drove him to help Carol, his clients, and most of all, himself. No matter what happened during this period in his life, it turned out to be his greatest gift.

When Carol apologized to Bob for falling ill, repeatedly saying, "I am so sorry," Bob did not assuage her worries but did the most profound thing. He thanked her. Not for getting sick, but for letting him do the work needed to be with her through her story arc. He thanked Carol for allowing him to love her, to hold her, to be there in the service of her illness. That moment was a catalyst for his change. It took Bob to another level, a deeper understanding, a clearer picture of who he was becoming in his new story.

We learned through this intense chapter of Bob's life that he came to an astonishing conclusion. Despite an incredibly challenging period, it proved to be the catalyst of extraordinary change. He discovered just how much more love he had inside of him—a love that he could both give and take. He was able, for the first time, in his humble opinion, to be compassionate. More importantly, he understood what it meant to be empathetic and to take care of somebody else to a degree he never thought possible. To consider Bob on the Emotional Intelligence scale, he was mastering Self-Awareness and Relationship Management. Embracing the mountainous challenge facing him and Carol tested his recognition of Self-Awareness. With a newfound confidence to embrace the jarring road ahead, he understood that his behavior would impact Carol's recovery and was determined to lead by example.

Self-Awareness	Self-Management	Social Awareness	Relationship Management
Assessment	Self-Control	Empathy	Conflict Management
Confidence	Transparency	Service to Others	Collaboration
	Adaptability		Influence

Bob gave intentional focus to the regulation of Relationship Management. Clearly expressing his feelings to Carol was just as important as his internal monologues and self-talk. When facing the mortality of a loved one, stress is amplified, weakening anyone's ability to be sensitive toward others as they shift into a mode of self-protection.

Since Bob wrote his new story, he often speaks of achieving on and off the court a state of equanimity—a mental calmness, composure, and the ability to maintain an even keel under the weight of enormous pressure. He also takes an occasional lesson out of the playbook of psychologist Mihaly Csikszentmihalyi, author of an excellent book called *Flow: The Psychology of Optimal Experience*. During World War II, Mihaly spent time in an Italian prison camp which had a profound effect on how he thought about human experiences. "As a child in the war I had seen something drastically wrong with how adults—the grown-ups I trusted—organized their thinking. I was trying to find a better system to order my life." He subsequently researched and wrote extensively about the concept of flow.

Imagine for a moment you are climbing a mountain. Your attention is focused on the movements of your body, the power of your muscles, the force of your lungs, and the feel of the ground beneath you. Living in the moment, you are fully absorbed in the present. Time stands still. Despite physical and mental fatigue, you barely notice. Whether you can classify it or not, you have experienced a mental state that Mihaly calls *flow*. Bob relies heavily on this model and strives to replicate it on all things on and off the tennis court.

Bob builds on Mihaly's premise that the flow state is random, but it doesn't need to be a rare event. "There are ways we can train ourselves to live closer to the flow state in a way we are more likely to fall into it." His premise and call to action include:

1. Identify people who have been in the flow state. For instance, a basketball player who made thirty shots in a row.

2. Think about your flow experiences. They are not as random as you think. Be familiar with how you got there.

3. Study and understand the conditions of your flow state. Understand how it feels. It allows you to change your story as you become more inclined to have automatic experiences.

Bob's point is that, if being in and achieving flow is part of your new story, you can build sufficient muscle memory. This will help to ensure it becomes a regular, not a random part of how you have chosen to "live the best story of your life" and sustain "lasting change."

His mission is to help everyone come to grips that "Life is a game, and you get to make the rules." His book started with the idea that we all need a New Story. By becoming the storyteller of your life, "Change can be easy, fun, and can happen in an instant." He urges everyone to "become your own coach." Most touching is what we learned from his book's Dedication about how to live the best story of *your* life:

"To Carol who, just by being Carol, showed me living the best story of my life was always possible, in good and difficult times, in victory and defeat, in joy and sadness, in both love and loss. That there is always light that shines through darkness. Her light shines on as I continue to live the best story of my life."[4]

CALL TO ACTION

To Serve

As Bob Litwin says in his book *Live the Best Story of Your Life,* "It's your life. You get to make the rules."

An interesting aspect of Stoicism is how death is often discussed in the same sentence as life. If death is part of "nature's will" the Stoics argue, it makes no more sense to fear it than it does the falling of leaves in autumn or their subsequent growth in the spring. The Stoics view death as a precondition for life, pointing out that life without death is not possible.

If that is the Stoic view on death, what do they say about how to live? Part of that question can be gleaned from the late Steve Jobs. The first time I watched his 2005 Stanford University commencement address on YouTube I was thunderstruck! Delivered with passion and purpose, I couldn't stop watching, wrote down every word, and memorized it. Many of his passages became part of my self-talk, especially

---

4   Litwin, Bob. *Live the best story of your life: A world champion's guide to lasting change.* New York: Hatherleigh, 2016.

when conflicted about something. When working through an issue with something or someone, I rely on my mental models referenced in Chapter 1 (Competence, Dignity, Trust). Adding to that, I combine them with Jobs' words of wisdom, certain the solution to my problem lies somewhere in that intersection. While his speech was brilliant at every turn, what struck me most about the life advice offered:

"Remembering that I'll be dead soon is the most important tool I've ever encountered to help me make the big choices in life.... Death is the destination we all share. No one has ever escaped it. And that is as it should be, because death is very likely the single best invention of life. It is life's change agent. It clears out the old to make way for the new. Right now, the new is you, but someday not too long from now, you will gradually become the old and be cleared away."[5]

He added later, "Your time is limited, so don't waste it living someone else's life. Don't be trapped by dogma—which is living with the results of other people's thinking. Don't let the noise of others' opinions drown out your inner voice. And most important, have the courage to follow your heart and intuition. They somehow already know what you truly want to become. Everything else is secondary."

To underscore his Stoic approach to life and death, his ultimate insight and advice from that speech is, "Remembering that you are going to die is the best way I know to avoid the trap of thinking you have something to lose."

---

5   Stanford. "Steve Jobs' 2005 Stanford Commencement Address (with Intro by President John Hennessy)." YouTube, May 14, 2008. https://www.youtube.com/watch?v=Hd_ptbiPoXM.

When you consider what advice Marcus Aurelius offers on living a life as you gradually become the old and make room for the new, his version of the Ten Commandments would be:

1. Live as if you died but were resuscitated, and every minute was a gift.

2. Every person you meet is an opportunity for kindness.

3. Be forgiving of others, but don't demand forgiveness for yourself.

4. Try to hold as few opinions as possible.

5. When caught in a bind, ask yourself, "What would Epictetus do?"

6. Practice good spending habits (keep in touch with poverty).

7. Always consider the worst-case scenario.

8. Keep a list of what you've learned from other people and remember to thank them along the way.

9. Wake up early every day—as early as you can.

10. If it is not right, don't do it. If it is not true, don't say it.

In his essay *On the Shortness of Life*, Seneca offers an urgent reminder that time is our most important resource. It is a guidebook on how to get control of your life and live to its fullest. He challenges us to beware of any activity that wastes time and to be vigilant not to put energy into unworthy pursuits.

Seneca describes the life of Augustus Caesar, considered one of the greatest Roman rulers in the history of the empire. Caesar often spoke that he longed to take a break from his responsibilities and sought to live a life of leisure. Seneca illuminates,

> *"This was the sweet, even if vain, consolation with which he would gladden his labors—that he would one day live for himself."*

Augustus ruled a vast domain but did not have control of his life. He did not have the luxury of spending time how he chose. Seneca explained, if the significance men strive for is a burden, they become buried in an avalanche of duties and concerns instead of living the life they want. In other words, it is better to live your life than to rule the world.

Make a list of your life rules. Then go out and live them.

CHAPTER 4

Nirupama Narayanaswamy: To Fulfill

"I am constant as the northern star, of whose true-fixed and resting quality there is no fellow in the firmament." William Shakespeare's *Julius Caesar*

Verb

1. Bring to completion or reality; achieve or realize (something desired, promised, or predicted).

2. Carry out (a task, duty, or role) as required, pledged, or expected.

For thousands of years, the North Star has been a guiding light for navigators and travelers, allowing them to sail the seas and cross the wilderness without getting lost. Formally known as Polaris, it has served as a beacon of hope and inspiration for countless humans. In astronomy, this point in space is called the north celestial pole and aligns with the earth's axis. As our planet spins, all stars seem to circle around it, while the North Star appears fixed. In astrology, the term refers to an individual's "north node" or destiny, the path to achieving fulfillment and purpose. Comparing himself to the North Star, Caesar boasts of his constancy,

THE MOMENT THAT DEFINES YOUR LIFE

commitment to the law, and refusal to waver under any persuasion.

Metaphorically speaking, the North Star is the personal mission statement. In Bill George's engaging book *True North: Discover Your Authentic Leadership*, he states, "True North is the internal compass that guides you successfully through life."

"Backed by intent, powered by intellect, driven by values," Nirupama Narayanaswamy, as she communicates on LinkedIn, is "a passionate Organizational Psychologist" with extensive experience "in project and people management." As she traversed her way to the United States from India, her diverse academic experience and professional expertise provided insights into people, processes, and systems to help individuals, teams, and organizations excel. She focuses on what matters most and assumes responsibility for activities that impact business, create visibility, and add value to any initiative she works on.

Nirupama sees her North Star clearly. It's a mission that seemed to be, for her, written in the stars. She follows it with purpose and passion integrating a high level of Emotional Intelligence reinforced by practices that would make Marcus Aurelius proud. She lives her life by three guiding principles:

1. **Purpose-driven and Impactful:** Focus on matters "bigger than me."

2. **Authenticity:** Her thoughts, words, and actions are aligned, genuine, and substantive.

3. **Dignity and Self-Respect:** The value she provides and the respect earned and granted to others are never taken for granted.

In her free time, she enjoys singing, drawing, watching documentaries, shows, and movies that are educational and purposeful, reading, and writing on topics that interest her. Professionally, she is an organizational effectiveness consultant for a global firm focused on strategy, technology, and business transformation. With an MBA from the Amrita School of Business in India and an MA from Columbia University in Social Organizational Psychology, she helps companies evaluate, develop, and implement plans to achieve optimal performance. An engineer by trade, her path to becoming an organizational psychologist is anything but a straight line. With several twists and turns, she continues to career climb committed to one immutable guideline: Stay true to her North Star and achieve a prosperous and fulfilling career through the lives she touches and the communities she builds.

EXPECTATION   **REALITY**

What happens, however, when the choices offered to you do not align with your North Star? What if someone else determines that path? How best to develop yourself when critical career decisions made are not yours?

Answers to these questions require cultural context to understand a model that explains how careers are often determined in India. In a 2013 article in *Asianscientist.com*, "India's engineers have gained worldwide attention for two reasons. First, graduates from the prestigious Indian Institutes of Technology (IITs), many of whom left to the US for higher education in the 1960s, began making a name for themselves in...business and technology....Second, *The New York Times* columnist Thomas Friedman and a few others began to write about...India's engineers in a flattering vein from the late 1990s onwards."[6]

Although engineering was already a popular area of study in India, it was bolstered by the global recognition of India's engineers and their success in the West. Consequently, it underscored that the IIT graduates had a recognizable brand name. Because countless successful alumni earned business degrees in the United States, an already-existing trend in India became routine. The mantra to many became, "Get a technical degree, go to business school, work for a big company, make lots of money, get featured in India's top newspapers (and perhaps even the *Wall Street Journal*) and live happily thereafter."

Flash forward to the twenty-first century. Consider that Google's CEO Sundar Pichai, Microsoft's Satya Nadella, and PepsiCo's Indra Nooyi followed this prescribed path and paved their way to fame and fortune. Add to this list another few dozen Indian trained engineers who became CEOs of

---

6   Pushkar. "Why Do Indian Students Take up Engineering Degrees?" Asian Scientist Magazine, June 2, 2013. https://www.asianscientist.com/2013/06/features/indian-students-engineering-degrees-2013/.

major global companies, and it is no wonder Indian parents want a similar educational arc for their children.

Nirupama's mother and father encouraged her to follow that path. Under the weight of parental expectations, she did what many ambitious, aspiring professionals in India do—listened to her parents and majored in electrical and electronic engineering. She subsequently worked in the IT industry as a software engineer. She also felt frustration and rage while acknowledging along the way that what she studied tirelessly had no intrinsic value. Unhappy and annoyed by doing work she was not passionate about, she thought, "There has to be another way." Any curiosity to be exposed to other professions was squashed. Her professional life was anything but enjoyable. She felt unable to apply other skills besides what was taught in the educational model of rote memorization. Up to that point she concluded, "I felt like a lifelong learner but had zero output or impact."

In 2011, while working at Europe's largest auto parts manufacturer, the moment arrived when she came to a fork in her career. Given the prospect of career advancement in the technical field, a big decision had to be made. Was she going to turn it down or continue to follow societal and parental expectations and take it? On the one hand, a career advancement meant moving to Germany to advance her career on a technical track. The prideful satisfaction of moving to one of the world's most advanced automobile engineering cultures was difficult to resist. It was safe, predictable, and would have brought her parents enormous pride. It was also soul-crushing! Nirupama felt a void that could only be filled by placing future career choices into her own hands. Neither her parents nor Indian compatriots could own this. From that day forward, the engineering degree was considered a part of her identity, but she did not let it define her. From now on, she declared, "I will invest in myself in the spirit of a more human/leadership-oriented career."

She subsequently left that company to pursue an MBA in India—not because she felt the need to follow the prescribed path or to live up to anyone else's expectations. She did it for one reason. It made her happy!

> *This was her next foundational moment. She made up her mind to defy Indian convention and advance on a platform of pride, fulfillment, and impact! She committed to becoming the master of her own fate, dismissing the status quo and owning her decisions, for better or worse.*

She then enrolled in an executive coaching program. It was the first time in her life someone asked, "What inspires you? What is your current reality? Where do you see yourself in five years?" These questions provided a structured and methodical way to clarify her goals and determine the means to achieve them. Finally, after years of feeling trapped in the lane of others' expectations, she aligned herself with self-inquiry and self-discovery. Aristotle's "knowing yourself is the beginning of all wisdom" became a part of her psyche.

Defying everyone else's expectations was life-altering. Until then, she was "never taught nor encouraged to think for herself." Nirupama committed, "If this doesn't make me happy, I am not going to do it. If it doesn't appeal to my heart and soul, I will not even consider it." She actively sought her happiness in defiance of culturally appropriate career aspira-tions. It led her down a path to become more centered and in charge of her domain. She started to ask herself hard-hitting questions, made her own decisions, and followed through on all of them.

> *If her decisions were wrong, she said, "I will bear*
> *the consequences." She accepted that and followed*
> *her heart.*

Nirupama changed the conversations she subsequently had with herself. That self-talk was leading her 180 degrees in a different direction. Asking herself, "What would con-tinue to make me happy?" she boarded a plane to New York City and embarked on a journey to earn another master's degree. This program of study, however, had little to do with engineering. If anything, she was now re-engineering her life approximately 8,400 miles from home. Any mention of sci-ence in this endeavor was preceded by the word *social*.

Adjective

1.   Tending to form cooperative and interdependent relationships with others.

2.   Living and breeding in organized communities, especially for the purpose of cooperation and mutual benefit.

Committed to following a path to fulfill her mind, body, and soul, Nirupama stepped onto the campus of Columbia University and never looked back. The MA in Social Organizational Psychology approaches issues from multiple perspectives, examining individuals, groups, and organizations. Their approach applies theory to practice, examining society's challenges and struggles head-on. Graduates head into a diverse and rapidly changing job market, learning the latest techniques that apply directly to their work and obtaining the capacity to make a difference in others' lives. Nirupama built on her leadership competencies and continued to think critically about contemporary issues facing individuals and companies. Refining the tools to assess, analyze, and implement organizational solutions, she learned to help clients face their most pressing problems and works collaboratively to solve them.

She subsequently joined a strategic consulting company which was a wonderful opportunity to work in a culture consistent with her core values of variety, fulfillment, and balance. Working with the world's top companies allows Nirupama to flex her skills across industries. Far from a job in coding and testing, she enjoys an exciting and rewarding career. She loves her work and life now, as it provides her the opportunity of making a significant difference in people's lives in a purposeful, meaningful way, while being her authentic self. This is ideal given Nirupama's burning desire to use her experience, work ethic, and drive in the service of others. All the movement that led Nirupama to her new reality are built on a foundation of cultural compatibility...to her company, her colleagues, and most importantly, to herself. Her current role is the perfect sweet spot for effectively leveraging her diverse academic background—analytical and logical (engineering mindset) with the ability of being able to connect the dots (business acumen) to positively impact people's lives (organizational psychology).

To refresh your memory on the four dimensions of Emotional Intelligence, it was clear that Nirupama had developed specific features of each:

Self-Awareness: The ability to focus on yourself and how your actions, thoughts, or emotions do or don't align with your internal standards.

Self-Management: The ability to regulate one's emotions, thoughts, and behaviors effectively in different situations.

Social Awareness: The ability to take the perspective of and empathize with others, including those from diverse backgrounds and cultures.

Relationship Management: A person's process of managing and optimizing interactions with friends, families, and colleagues.

Self-Awareness	Self-Management	Social Awareness	Relationship Management
Assessment	Self-Control	Empathy	Conflict Management
Confidence	Transparency	Service to Others	Collaboration
	Adaptability		Influence

Describing the experience at her firm, "For the first time in a long while, I feel extremely fulfilled." Not just from a paycheck or promotion but to feel in full control and live so many moments that fill not only her mind but also her heart and soul. Relying on certain engineering skills learned in college, she thankfully figured out how to transfer many of them and apply those that are measurable and effective. She is not just engineering her career transformation but is on a path to help others engineer theirs.

NIRUPAMA'S EMOTIONAL INTELLIGENCE DEVELOPMENT

Through a continuous series of frustrations in her life in India, the discontent caused her to reject external expectations and direct all her attention inward. Self-aware that she was lacking fulfillment, she found the courage to overcome social pressure. She acted out of Bob Litwin's playbook and said,

"It's my life. I get to make the rules."

She clearly saw the gap between what she was doing and the boundless potential trapped inside. The defining moment was a stunning realization that the quality of her life was not to be condensed to a representation of the material she learned in school. Checking boxes defined by others would not equate to her happiness, so she rewrote her own, demonstrating a thorough understanding of her Self-Awareness and Self-Management.

She often speaks of the difference between working while "fully present"—mind, body, spirit—and the consequences of being "partially present." Despite money, fame, and/or whatever accomplishments, "Fulfillment only happens when you are aligned and fully present at the intersection of what you love and what you are good at."

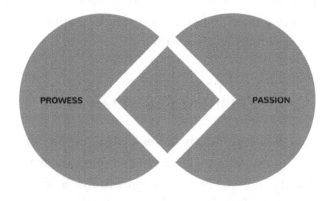

Nirupama exemplified the spirit of acting in congruence with her values. If it does not bring happiness, count her out. If any circumstances cause her to question her values, they are not negotiable. Handling changes flexibly and pursuing goals despite obstacles and setbacks came naturally. While she was always assessing the next opportunity, despite unhappiness, she did not stop to lament about her circumstances. She persevered and continued to work, seeking positions that aligned with her passion and purpose...and that she found fulfilling.

NIRUPAMA AND THE STOIC PHILOSOPHY

Stoics assert that the ideal life is one in harmony with nature. They underscore the need to sustain an attitude of calm indifference toward external events. It began in Greece and was founded by Zeno of Citium, who taught at the Painted Stoa in Athens, hence the name Stoicism. The Stoa Poikile, or "Painted Porch," was erected in the fifth-century BC and is located on the north side of the Ancient Agora of Athens. One of the most famous sites in ancient Athens, it owes its fame to the paintings and loot left behind from a variety of wars. But the work of the early Stoics is, for the most part, lost. Consequently, the Roman Stoics salvaged what they could and have been prolific promoters of this philosophy ever since.

In the *Handbook of Epictetus*, a manual of ethical advice written in the second century, the definition of this philosophy is clear and concise. According to Epictetus,

> *"The chief task in life is simply this: to identify and separate matters so that I can say clearly to myself which are externals not under my control, and which have to do with the choices I actually control. Where then do I look for good and evil? Not to uncontrollable externals, but within myself to the choices that are my own."*

Stoicism holds that the key to a happy life is the cultivation of a sound mental state. In what has become a manual for the Stoics to practice, he describes two founding principles which apply so powerfully to how Nirupama guides her life.

- In the first, Epictetus asserts we don't control what happens to us and cannot control what the people around us say or do. The only thing that we control is how we think about things and the judgments we make.

- In the second, it is neither things nor circumstances that upset us but how we think about them. What may seem horrible to one person may be a matter of indifference to someone else or perhaps welcomed. It is the judgments we make that introduce value into the equation. It is those value judgments that generate our emotional responses.

In short, the most important practices in Stoic philosophy are differentiating between what we can change and what we can't. What we have influence over and what we do not.

Like a seasoned Stoic, Nirupama accepted as neutral the pain that comes with decisions that defy stereotypes and the status quo. While feeling others' judgments that her decisions were shortsighted or lacked good judgment, she was willing to pay that price to think and act independently and in her best interests. She chose to view all that interference as fuel necessary to forge her own path of hope, happiness, and love.

The paradox of Stoicism, as Epictetus proclaims, is that we have almost no control over anything, yet we have potentially complete control over our happiness. Nirupama understood that, despite others' best intentions, the capacity to decide her life plan had to live in one place…her heart. Once she made up her mind that happiness is at the top of life's hierarchy, decisions would reflect the courage and conviction to leverage all circumstances into a life that only she was destined to lead.

TOOLS YOU CAN IGNITE TO LIVE A STOIC LIFE

When I first discovered this philosophy, I was skeptical. Everything I read seemed to oversimplify everything. Many in my circle were facing daunting challenges, striving to resolve conflicts that overwhelmed and exhausted them. How can thinking differently help someone who is struggling with life's most basic needs? The Stoics did not dismiss this and acknowledged life can be difficult and taxing. Seneca suffered exile and buried many friends and loved ones. It was one thing to say, "I'm not going to let these external events affect me." Quite another to follow through and act as the *Handbook of Epictetus* articulates. Consequently, the Stoics developed a series of exercises designed to incorporate practices into their daily lives.

- Seneca recommends taking stock at the end of each day. Note when you become irritated by something trivial or act indignantly in response to someone who did not deserve your wrath. Note the impulses and mistakes made. Take three deep breaths. If you could rewind that event, what would it look like? What would you have done differently? Instead of making a bold statement, resume the conversation with a question. For example, "I appreciate where you are coming from, but I don't understand. Why did you say that?" We often rush to judgment when under duress. In the heat of that moment, we exclaim the first thing that comes to mind rather than taking time to formulate an answer that is positive and productive.

- Marcus Aurelius had another approach. He reminded himself daily that he would encounter lots of angry, impatient, ungrateful people throughout the day. Through his daily meditations, he trained the mind to show up in a friendly manner, noting he would be less likely to respond in kind. He also considered that most people do not intentionally act that way. They were victims of their own mistaken judgments and would benefit mightily from learning Stoic practices.

- Another tactic is to occasionally remind ourselves that the world does not revolve around us. Aurelius regularly reflected on the vastness of the universe and the infinity of time to put his brief life into a wider context. He recognized our lives are simply moments placed within a broader worldview. It would be ludicrous to expect the universe to bend to our will.

Nirupama has spent years embracing life's ebbs and flows that transcend nationality, culture, and career choices. With every interaction, she opened her mind, opened her heart, and opened the door to life's endless possibilities. As she considered her old story and sat down to write a new one, I couldn't help but notice the compelling word choices she wrote to me as we prepared for this interview:

> I...
>
> *...am valued and admired for my character, brains, and beauty.*
>
> *...am independent, have a mind of my own, possess the courage to stand up, speak up, and value what I believe.*
>
> *...am a source of inspiration to everyone, particularly women, and challenge stereotypes.*
>
> *... live a life of authenticity, with a version of truth, given my cross-cultural identity and experiences, based on whatever I've learnt from others around me.*
>
> *...am taking care of myself physically, financially, emotionally, and mentally and on self-love and self-care every step of the way.*
>
> *...am focused and committed to my goals, visualize everyday about my desired future state/vision for future, and let go of limiting beliefs, becoming a better version of myself.*

...am thoroughly intentional/purposeful about everything I do, where the intent matches the outcome/impact. My daily activities reflect my overall priorities and goals.

...am comfortable about "being" as much as "doing."

I hope her story arc makes the most diehard Stoics recognize they left us a powerful, persuasive, and actionable legacy. Although they did not develop this philosophy with Nirupama Narayanaswamy in mind, it is wonderful to watch her contribute so much good to the world using these principles. I hope her inspiring story will continue to ignite others to climb to the top of their proverbial mountains as she continually redefines what it means to fulfill.

CALL TO ACTION

To Fulfill

To many philosophers, fulfillment is realizing one's deepest desires. Called "eudaimonia" in Greek, Stoicism became an extensive body of interdependent doctrines that all support each other on the path to fulfillment. The philosophy was divided into:

- Logic: The study of reasoning
- Ethics: The study of morality
- Physics: The study of natural phenomena

Fulfillment is what the Stoics assert leads to happiness—always living a life where you "do the right thing because that is the right thing to do." We can make sense of this idea with a distinction between outcome and process.

Many people find fulfillment in things associated with outcomes—results attained given goals and objectives. Naturally, human beings incline toward the pursuit of certain outcomes, including wealth, meaningful relationships, and excellent health. The Stoics assert that fulfillment does not come from getting them but on that path to attainment. You achieve it in the process, not in the outcome. This is the true origin of fulfillment—doing something to do it well. It is why we take up hobbies. Some grow vegetables; others play tennis. Whatever it is, the same principles apply; doing a thing simply to do it well fulfills us.

The trick is to live every aspect of our lives that way. If you want to know how to find fulfillment at work, it is not just to make a living or advance your career. You will pay your bills and even build wealth. However, that is not where fulfillment finds its way.

GOAL- OR PROCESS-ORIENTED? TIPS TO OPTIMIZE THE PATH TO FULFILLING OUTCOMES

Like a good mountaineer, focus on the next step of the process, not the last.

The Stoics assert we must strive to make process excellence the priority. Stick to the basics. Athletes are reminded of this daily to avoid getting into bad habits. Do your best to always do the right thing. Resist the impulse to look too far ahead on any project. Many people worry about something that has not even happened. Often that anxiety comes from procrastinating or a lack of preparation that leads to guilt. There is discipline to process orientation and consequences when that discipline breaks down. Hence, more energy is focused on something unproductive.

Conversely, to set process-oriented goals, it is best to ask a different set of questions versus result-oriented goals. With result orientation, you consider the effectiveness, impact, and relevance of those goals. With process orientation, it is the path, the state you are in while you're pursuing them that matters.

Results-Oriented:

- Focus on meeting your objectives
- Strive to make progress despite constraints
- Deal well with ambiguity

Process-Oriented:

- Work in established systems and structures
- Focus on the journey not the destination
- Discipline to stay the course despite obstacles

Process, then, is the repeatable approach to solving a problem or getting the results you want. Outcome alone as the measure of success is not enough. As you strive to get more things accomplished, pay attention to *how*, not just *what*, you do. If you are motivated by the process, you pay more attention to the systems, principles, and methods for getting there. In mountaineering, it is "keep your head down and climb."

People who swear by the process believe the results will take care of themselves if the process is rigorous.

I have worked with people on both sides of this spectrum and concluded the two choices are not mutually exclusive. However, the most effective people lean to the side of process-orientation and tend to be Stoic (whether they know it or not) in their methods. Why?

1. **Being process-driven allows us to detach from our emotions:** Ineffectively controlling our emotions is often the biggest impediment to achievement.

2. **Success is not one big leap:** It is the culmination of many tiny steps: This concept has been studied countless times in the books we read on maximizing human performance. Change is incremental. Whether climbing mountains, losing weight, or writing a book. When process driven, you focus on tiny daily victories and how they sum up and pay off over time.

3. **It is easy to get discouraged when you focus on what you do not have:** There is an old proverb I learned long ago that states, "The more tightly I grasp at things, the easier they are to fall out of my hands." The implication: Detach yourself from the goal. Don't even think about it. Just keep climbing. That doesn't lessen your desire to reach the summit but implies all your energy is directed at each step right in front of you. It means being present, in the moment, for what is needed to stay on course. Keep your head down and your mind clear.

Tips to Highlight a Process-Orientation:

- When faced with a problem or situation, don't look far beyond. Search for the nearest relevant set of steps, policies, instructions, guidelines, rules, or regulations.

- To set and manage expectations when others are involved, stay true to structure. For instance, construct a clearly defined agenda, start and end precisely on time, and have a clear call to action when the meeting is over. I am not a big believer in allowing wiggle room in meetings. If something emerges that may be worth examining but throws the agenda off track, it is best taken offline. There is nothing more soul-crushing than watching meetings go off the rails and end in stalemate, uncertainty, and a hastily communicated call to action.

When you consider Nirupama's journey of twists and turns, one element is unwavering. She stayed true to her values and made up her mind not to capitulate to anyone else's expectations. Integrating the process mind of an engineer with the strategic mind of a consultant, she continually reminds herself of the need to stay hyper-focused. In her personal mission statement, she speaks of the importance of a healthy mind and body, doing everything with intention, and taking life one step at a time.

Her story is an inspiration to anyone considering the discomfort of change. Integrating the powerful tools of

Emotional Intelligence and Stoicism, she learned, sometimes the hard way, that to change anything, it was critical to first change herself. While the outcome did not always seem obvious with every change, I am certain that if she and Marcus Aurelius were sharing a meal, his insightful and actionable words would keep her grounded and always ready for the next series of unpredictable events. More importantly, they would underscore her generosity and desire to make a difference in the lives of others by leading her own change and inspiring others to do the same. To quote the great Emperor Aurelius, "Observe constantly that all things take place by change and accustom thyself to consider that the nature of the Universe loves nothing so much as to change the things which are, and to make new things like them."

CHAPTER 5

Jamie Bassel:
To Adjust

Noun

1. Alter or move something slightly to achieve the desired fit, appearance, or result.

2. Assess (loss or damages) when settling an insurance claim.

3. What chiropractors do when treating their patients.

Daniel David Palmer immigrated to the United States from Canada in the nineteenth century. Anyone who felt ill back then and asked him the reason why, he likely would have responded with great conviction, "The human body has an ample supply of natural healing power transmitted through the nervous system. If any organ is affected by illness, it must not be receiving its normal nerve supply." He called this a spinal misalignment or subluxation. Consequently, he would have done what chiropractors do and treated you with his hands to accelerate the healing process.

Palmer regarded chiropractic as a form of manipulating the body to reestablish the nerve supply. He is thus credited with giving the first chiropractic treatment in 1895. He subsequently founded The Palmer College of Chiropractic in Davenport, Iowa, two years later and passionately led a movement to restore good health to millions of people. Flash forward to 2023, and there are forty-three schools worldwide and over 100,000 chiropractors.

The word *chiropractic* derives from the Greek words *cheir* (meaning "hand") and *praktos* (meaning "done"), or literally, done by hand. While hand-based healing methods can be traced to antiquity, it was not until the early 1900s that the profession in the United States emerged. According to Johns Hopkins, "Chiropractic medicine is based on the link between the alignment of the spine and the function of the body. A core tenet...is that the body has the ability to heal itself given proper support."[7] Treatment typically involves lying prone on a special table while the chiropractor uses his or her hands to realign the spine.

Jamie Bassel immigrated to the United States from Canada in the late twentieth century. After studying anatomy at Montreal's McGill University, he was inspired by what he learned about aligning and restoring the human nerve supply. He subsequently started his career in research at the University of Pennsylvania, then headed to Los Angeles to study chiropractic medicine.

Twenty-five years later, his New York City–based practice provides breakthrough pain treatment. Dr. Bassel's goal is to relieve any kind of discomfort and help others live healthy and productive lives. Uniquely trained and experienced in

---

7   "Chiropractic Medicine." Johns Hopkins Medicine. https://www.hopkins medicine.org/health/wellness-and-prevention/chiropractic-medicine.

diagnosing musculoskeletal problems, he uses his hands to apply a controlled, sudden force to a spinal joint known as a chiropractic adjustment.

As his practice grew, Jamie started consulting as a medical examiner with a panel of distinguished specialists in many fields of medicine to ensure patients nationwide receive appropriate attention and care. Augmenting his circle of competence, he often provides expert testimony in legal cases that require his extensive experience.

To meet Jamie is to recognize you are in the presence of a highly skilled professional with exceptional communication skills. When seeking to understand the source of your bodily pain, he first examines you. Then, he explains in clear and concise language the source of your discomfort. Relying on his thoroughly trained mind (and hands), he "adjusts" you to initiate the healing process. He has treated thousands of patients through the years and is valued for the enormous dedication he brings to the art and science of his craft. Effectively relying on characteristics associated with both sides of the human brain, Jamie integrates incomparable prowess and passion.

But what if...

- Dr. Bassel is presented with a case whose remedy is not in his domain?

- The diagnosis and subsequent treatment do not resemble anything he learned in school?

- The patient in question is his firstborn child?

One of Jamie's moments came to light just after his son Zakary was born. Delivered via cesarian section, he was unable to be nursed by his mother despite repeated attempts. The sucking reflex, a natural process of feeding the baby, was hampered. Eventually, it prompted caution and concern that something was wrong. For the next month, while Jacqueline was recovering from the C-section, they coped for weeks trying to make sense of the circumstances. Finally, under the care of a neonatologist and a genetic test, Zak was diagnosed with Prader-Willi (PRAH-dur VIL-e) syndrome.

According to the Mayo Clinic, it "is a rare genetic disorder...caused by an error in one or more genes. Although the exact mechanisms responsible have not been identified, the problem lies in the genes located in a particular region of chromosome 15....[It] results in" several "physical, mental, and behavioral" issues. "A key feature of Prader-Willi syndrome is a constant sense of hunger that usually begins at about 2 years of age....Best managed by a team approach, various specialists" help "manage symptoms of this complex disorder, reduce the risk of developing complications, and improve the quality of life" for the patient. Additional "signs and symptoms...present from birth" include diminished muscle tone, distinct facial features, and low responsiveness.[8] During early childhood and throughout their lives, features include excessive food cravings, weight gain, and delayed motor development.

---

8   Mayo Clinic Staff. "Prader-Willi Syndrome." Mayo Clinic,
      January 31, 2018. https://www.mayoclinic.org/diseases-conditions/
      prader-willi-syndrome/symptoms-causes/syc-20355997.

Jamie explained Prader-Willi using a visual metaphor to help me see it more clearly. "Imagine you are sitting in one of the sections at a stadium, and several seats are missing. Think of those gaps as genetic material that is lacking from the chromosome. As the body matures, critical information is absent, changing the way Zak will develop as he grows up."

In the Neonatal Intensive Care Unit for approximately six months, bringing Zak home became a daily balancing act. With Jacqueline recovering from abdominal surgery and Zak "constantly teetering on the brink of catastrophe," Jamie had his hands full. He compared the experience to "being stuck in the middle of an ocean without a life raft—flailing, doing everything possible to keep my head above water." His daily mission was, "Hold it all together for the sake of my family."

News of the diagnosis and the uncertainty of what followed was an immense amount for him to digest. He thought, *How am I going to manage this?* To learn more about Prader-Willi, he reviewed their website to glean information and clue him into what to expect. "With every line I read, it became more apparent we were in for substantial challenges of dealing with this multisystemic disorder." He was feeling sorry for himself, constantly wondering why.

Here was a seasoned, successful medical practitioner trained to treat people who came to him in pain and left his office on a path to recovery and good health. Many, like me, became lifelong patients. With Zak, he felt helpless, unable to care for him the way he had for countless others. Consequently, he was engaged in a proverbial seesaw between his heart, where he felt pity, and his mind, where he was keenly aware of the evidence. The father in him was all heart. The Doctor of Chiropractic was all mind, trained to treat and cure what ails others. How would he get out of this funk and help his son?

THE TURNING POINT

"Even the longest journey must begin where you stand."

Laozi

In a moment of reflection, he recalled another absorbing moment that the neontologist said to him, which helped him come to terms with Zak's diagnosis.

"If you pour all of your energy into your child, you'd be amazed at the things that can occur."

Jamie was at a crossroads, thinking to himself, "I can wallow in pity, but that does not change the facts." Saddled with information overload and dazed at the road ahead, Jamie kept asking himself what to do. In a powerful moment of clarity, one person came to mind. He contacted a childhood friend named Scott Wright, who was diagnosed with cerebral palsy during his childhood. Jamie remembered Scott's parents as a guiding force for good in his life. They encouraged him to be the best possible version of himself as they loved, supported, and believed in him. While it may have come as no surprise to his parents, Scott became the director of Johns Hopkins Bayview Division of General Internal Medicine.

When Jamie called him to describe what was happening with Zak, Scott howled at him unexpectedly and said,

> *"Get your head out of his ass and devote all your attention to the kid who needs you so desperately."*

This moment was far more powerful than news of the diagnosis. Although neither the self-pity nor self-loathing immediately disappeared, Scott's convincing call to action gave him a sense of purpose and direction he was desperately grasping for...and that only one other offered.

> *Scott threw Jamie the life preserver he needed while treading water in the middle of that ocean.*

That phone conversation was the moment that defined the rest of Jamie's life. It provided clarity that forced him to recognize it was time to put his head down and focus on the things that really mattered—Zak. This moment set Jamie on a path to create the best possible life for his son and establish an infrastructure to optimize his care and support.

Jamie was reminded time and again that life is filled with unanticipated obstacles. When confronted, it is a burden if you freeze in your tracks and feel immobilized. Or you can choose to view it as an opportunity. In retrospect, Jamie feels he was lucky to be made aware of his son's news early on. He acknowledged the timing was an occasion to care for and provide for Zak. While any parent could have treated only the problem...it was also an opportunity to get ahead of this and determine a plan to foster his son's growth.

Jamie also recognized that there are things within us that we are asked to summon. His response to Scott lends credence to the adage, "Where you focus, your energy follows." Jamie acknowledged that the initial attention on himself was misguided and unproductive. He feels "Anyone can be surprised to find the drive needed to overcome what at first seems impossible."

> Once you come to terms with your truth and face
> it honestly, you unlock and deliver unanticipated,
> immense power.

Jamie could have easily folded under the weight of that diagnosis, given so many unknowns. If he had, it likely would have set Zak on a very different path.

After the phone call with Scott, Jamie started down his new path. A trail that ultimately led him to build a powerful support team of multifactorial medical professionals for Zak's wellbeing. Add to that a loving and supportive family, and thankfully Zak is thriving. Jamie thus became involved in the local chapter of the Prader-Willi Alliance of New York, furthering his understanding of what other families were experiencing for their children with the same diagnosis. He subsequently created a nonprofit entity (501c3) called Zak's Promise: Progress with Support, Inc. to raise awareness and research funding for Prader-Willi syndrome.

Jamie became the father Zak needed him to be.

Initially, he had many preconceived notions about what it meant to be a father. Yet, his ideals were challenged by unexpected circumstances. Consequently, this was Jamie Bassel, Doctor of Chiropractic's most important adjustment—himself. He redefined what it meant to be a dad. He states those defining experiences forced him to slow down, to stop and smell the roses more often. Given all these considerations, "You tend to be a bit more humbled in the way that you approach things," he says. Placing his hands on Zak would not change the diagnosis. Having dedicated so many years to healing the sick with his hands, who knew that, with all that training, what was required was a reeducation and a new skill set to treat his son?

Jamie embodied several Stoic characteristics throughout that moment. He acknowledged, "This was not in my control." Jamie learned through these trials and tribulations to develop himself by building on the integration of heart and mind.

> *"Accept the things to which fate binds you, and love the people with whom fate brings you together, but do so with all your heart."*
>
> Marcus Aurelius

Given the three disciplines of Stoicism: Perception, Action, and Will, Jamie embodied each in sequence. Once he perceived that Zak's diagnosis was not a burden but an opportunity to prepare and guide his life accordingly, his mindset changed. All actions subsequently were done in the service of Zak's good health, disconnected from the pity and pain which appeared at the onset. Third, it constantly tested Jamie's will and helped him to see things differently. He thus came to terms with what it meant to be a husband, a health practitioner, and most of all...a dad!

> *"You have the power over your mind—not outside events. Realize this, and you will find strength."*
>
> Marcus Aurelius

Jamie knew if he did not step up to the proverbial plate, it could have been catastrophic for Zak. He was open-minded about where he could improve throughout Zak's care and paid attention to ensuring the best outcomes as the journey unfolded. As Epictetus was fond of saying, "Circumstances do not make the man, they only reveal him to himself."

On the Emotional Intelligence scale, Self-Management was the predominant focus of Jamie's growth. He learned to continually keep his disruptive emotions and impulses in check (for himself, his wife, and his son). His mindset continued to act and adjust, consistent with his values of being the father Zak needed him to be. He never relented on his goal of being a great dad despite the obstacles in front of him.

Self-Awareness	Self-Management	Social Awareness	Relationship Management
Assessment	Self-Control	Empathy	Conflict Management
Confidence	Transparency	Service to Others	Collaboration
	Adaptability		Influence

Regarding Relationship Management, Zak's circumstances initiated introductions and friendships beyond any measure Jamie could have expected. In trying times, you find out who your friends are. His reconnection with Scott was a powerful moment of candor, clarity, and tough love. Scott communicated what Jamie's friendship meant to him through one act of simple and actionable advice. He did what good friends do. He spoke the truth, prompting Jamie to acknowledge it, face it, and manage it.

In addition, Jamie was introduced to and cultivated a wide array of medical professionals whose expertise, generosity, and encouragement were guiding lights in Zak's development. Lastly, consider the taxing nature of what happens to a marriage when tested to its limits. It is challenging enough, given life's routine pressures, to keep a marriage and family intact physically, mentally, and spiritually. It's quite another when dealing with a series of events of which there is no precedence. It is hard enough with a newborn to endure sleepless nights and respond to unfamiliar cries. Although Jamie may not have been conscious of it, he was building a mental fortress, as well as conditioning himself and learning to deal with adversity on a scale he never have could imagined.

Finally, Self-Awareness was on display the moment Zak was born. Jamie walked a fine line during those demanding times, assessing the crushing weight of the diagnosis that could have sent him plunging into a dark place. But Jamie didn't do that. He was aware of the need to manage his emotions for the sake of Zak, Jacqueline, and anyone who touched their lives. Every action with Zak was intentional, guided with purpose, and helped Jamie continue to redefine what it meant to be a father.

Social psychologists have long recognized the roles head and heart play in our personal and professional lives. In 1995 Daniel Goleman brought Emotional Intelligence to the mainstream and provided a platform to examine the influence of feelings and emotions on us and the world around us. The sum of what we think, feel, and act is what people talk about when they talk about us. In the words of the great psychologist Carl Jung, "I am not what happened to me, I am what I choose to become."

Lastly, modern psychology acknowledges the importance of adjusting behavior in response to events that occur all around us. Abe Arkoff, author of *Psychology and Personal Growth*, defines adjustment as "the condition of a person who can adapt to changes in their physical, occupational, and social environment. Adjustment also refers to the behavioral process of balancing conflicting needs and/or needs challenged by environmental obstacles. The 'adjustment as a process' theory articulates that, since the moment we are born, humans are in a constant state of adjustment."

While Zak has adjusted very well to daily life since birth, he is happy to call Jamie his dad. While Jamie continues to adjust patients and himself to the events around him, he expresses equal gratitude for being able to call Zak his son. As Zak and his sister Lily have defined his role as a father, he follows their lead to help him and Jacqueline stay grounded.

CALL TO ACTION

To Adjust

Some common synonyms of adjust are *accommodate*, *adapt*, and *reconcile*. Two thousand years ago Marcus Aurelius wrote:

> *"Every part of me then will be reduced by change into some part of the universe, and that again will change into another part of the universe, and so on forever."*

He continued in *Meditations* to beg many questions, which included:

- What can take place without change?
- What, then, is more pleasing or more suitable to the universal nature?
- Can anything else that is useful be accomplished without it?

The Stoics knew firsthand that change is hard, and we often suffer anticipating it. When uncertain of an outcome, needless energy is expended, worrying whether or not the adjustments will be effective. Anticipation of change can lead to overthinking, doubting our ability to cope, and making mountains out of molehills. Fearing the unknown often ignites a massive amount of anxiety despite that, according to Heraclitus, the Greek philosopher, "Change is the only constant."

Resistance to change is understandable. The brain works hard to maintain its habits. It takes a lot of time and energy to break them, given the comfort and safety of living in a predictable world. If you can accept change as an intrinsic part of nature and hold yourself accountable to adjust to changing circumstances, it will dramatically improve your resilience and strength to face whatever the world throws at you. It is therefore the nature of the universe to embrace the capacity to adjust.

Here are some mindset development tips when faced with the need to adjust anything:

1. Loss, be it money, a friend, or time, is neither good nor bad. Our perception of the event(s) determines which one. The suffering experienced is an ability to accept it and adjust to the changing circumstances.

2. Control is an illusion. Through control, many find great comfort. We like to think we exert a great deal of control over all things in our world. However, Epictetus believed that things in our control are opinion, pursuit, and desire. Not in our control are body, property, and reputation. Reverting to the need for process orientation, you control the inputs, not the outcomes.

"Demand not that things happen as you wish, but wish them to happen as they do, and you will go on well." Epictetus

I. Examine your expectations and adjust if you believe they are unreasonable. As Yuval Noah Harari, sounding like a Stoic, wrote in his brilliant book *Sapiens*, "Happiness does not really depend on objective conditions of either wealth, health or even community. Rather, it depends on the correlation between objective conditions and subjective expectations."

We can use the concepts of control, expectation, and acceptance to change how we perceive the world and become more resilient to its hardships and challenges. But this is not a panacea. It requires everyone to take responsibility to develop mindset tools to live a happier life. To accept things we cannot control, time and energy are focused on the things you can adjust—you!

Similarly, accept that unrealistic expectations cause grief. By adjusting them, you create more realistic prospects to confront the issues in front of you. We are all part of a cycle that requires a series of continual adjustments. Resist change, and it threatens to unearth the life routines you worked so hard to establish. Or, learn to accept it as a natural part of your existence and become resilient in the face of adversity.

CHAPTER 6

Anthony Sicuranza Jr.:
To Compensate

Verb

1. Give (someone) something, typically money, in recognition of loss, suffering, or injury incurred, recompense.

2. Reduce or counteract (something unwelcome or unpleasant) by exerting an opposite force or effect.

3. Attempt to conceal or offset one's shortcomings by the exaggerated exhibition of qualities regarded as desirable.

In the early 1900s, on a dig in what is now southern Iraq, archaeologists unearthed a tablet considered to be one of the earliest examples of human writing. Dating to 3300 BC, Alison George at *NewScientist* explained, "The tablet displays a human head eating from a bowl. Scratch marks across its surface denote the amount of beer rations paid to a worker. Historians theorize this was the world's oldest pay slip, implying the concept of employer and employee was in place five thousand years ago."[9] As Gus O'Donnell, former head of the British Civil Service told the BBC in 2010, "What's amazing for me is that this is a society where the economy is in its first stages. here is no currency, no money. So how do they get around that? Well, the symbols tell us that they have used beer—beer glorious beer, I think that is absolutely tremendous; there is no liquidity crisis here, they are coming up with a different way of getting around the problem of the absence of a currency."[10] The beer-for-work custom is also evident in ancient Egypt, where pyramid workers were paid four to five liters per day. Historical records from other civilizations show that laborers were most often compensated with food, shelter, and other necessities.

In ancient Rome, there was another valuable commodity referred to as "white gold." This barter system was going strong in 50 BC as the soldiers were paid in salt. Demand was driven by how important it was to preserve food, especially meat and fish. Consequently, the word *salary* derives from the Latin *salarium*, which means "salt money." Hence, if anyone ever says, "You are worth your salt," take it as a compliment.

Fast-forward to the Commercial Revolution in the sixteenth century and the emergence of national economies based on trade. Salaries began to look like what we recognize today, with employees paid for their time and/or things produced. Back then, currency was acceptable as bartering faded away. When large organizations like the East India Company

9   George, Alison. "The World's Oldest Paycheck Was Cashed in Beer." New Scientist, June 27, 2016. https://www.newscientist.com/article/2094658-the-worlds-oldest-paycheck-was-cashed-in-beer/.
10 Ibid.

emerged, organizations started to compensate employees differently, often with a portion of company profits.

When you consider the number of professions that evolved through the years, engineer, firefighter, and plumber may come to mind. Each of them is relied on to create something or otherwise fix a problem. We value the depth of their training and depend on them as needed. I am willing to bet there is one profession that does not surface when you ask your son or daughter, "What do you want to be when you grow up?" The response you are not likely to hear is "compensation analyst." Although people who practice this profession are not the subject of primetime television shows, it is a critical profession for companies of all shapes and sizes.

Throughout the twentieth century, American workers witnessed an evolution in compensation practices. For starters, changes in methods of pay have usually been stimulated by some form of imbalance caused by a crisis or demographic shift. No greater calamity was experienced than the Great Depression, a watershed event in how employers paid their workers. Growth in unionization and an increase in the number of working women, among other factors, have contributed to changes in pay practices. Payment for labor services has evolved from just wages to sophisticated compensation "packages" that involve a variety of elements. Today, benefits continue to develop, as variable features like family leave, profit sharing, and stock options become even more important. Consider when you...

- Receive a paycheck deposited directly to your bank account, how did it get there?

- Want to develop your public speaking skills to deliver a compelling presentation to your boss, who in your company comes to mind?

- Are focused on career advancement and want a Human Resources partner to assess, monitor, and cultivate your leadership competencies, who do you call?

Supporting Google's journey with 170,000 employees is Anthony Sicuranza, Jr. When you review his LinkedIn profile, below the headshot you see: *Dad/Compensation @ Google*. Rarely on a professional social media site have I seen someone lead with a parental reference. Sporting a company shirt and a big smile, those two entries say a lot about Anthony's views of work-life balance. He is a results-oriented Googler who flourishes in driving organizational development at one of the world's most prolific companies. As a people-first leader who has orchestrated countless Human Resources programs, he is a master of compensation design...and a great dad.

Anthony's moment can be distilled into a revelatory event when he learned to listen and act by removing his ego, biases, and blind spots. Powerfully tied to the four Emotional Intelligence pillars, what occurred at that moment, and who he has become is best understood when you examine the arc of his self-perceived failures.

REDEFINING WHAT IT MEANS TO COMPENSATE

In high school, Anthony's life path was straightforward—surviving the dreadful high school classes and going to work at his father's mechanic shop. Lofty ambitions and big dreams were not part of his mindset. Unfortunately, when his dad's business suddenly closed, Anthony's plan dissolved with it. He subsequently toiled away in a variety of blue-collar jobs, but nothing stuck. Lacking strong role models with no exposure to an inspiring or influential leader, those gaps continually pushed him away as he wondered if there were any other possibilities. But the continual job-hopping and lack of career engagement began to weigh heavily on him. The self-perceived notions of "I am a failure" replayed like a broken record. His internal battles raged with no resolution. Unlike his peers committed to their education and professional development, skipping from job to job became the norm. As he anxiously sought to find his place in the world, career choices and lack of financial resources were constantly in question, further eroding his confidence.

In the fight to find his sense of self, Anthony gave thought to the stability that comes with a career in public service. With completed applications in a variety of state and municipal agencies, his local police department in Mount Vernon, New York, was the only organization to consider his candidacy. Despite his longing for a fresh start, he was admittedly "in a bad mental state." Depressed, half employed, and struggling to sustain healthy habits, he felt hopeless.

However, he passed the police written exam and qualified for the next stage in the appraisal process, a test of his physical fitness. Anthony was not in shape, but he recognized that this was his best opportunity to make something of himself. Join the police force, serve and protect, and retire with a pension. "This is my shot, and I don't intend to blow it," he told himself. Tired of feeling so despondent, the next move represented far more than a steady paycheck. It had to do with his self-respect. Since the stakes were too high to fail, he used what little money he had saved and hired a personal trainer. He recognized the path to cure these ills was to prepare for the intense evaluation that stood between him and his measure of self-worth. Feeling mentally and physically equipped, the date finally arrived.

Passing this test required performing at least thirty-seven sit-ups in sixty seconds. To qualify, his shoulders had to touch the mat for each repetition. The good news: thirty-seven sit-ups. The bad news: His shoulders did not touch the mat on one of them, reducing the count to thirty-six. Anthony failed the physical and did not qualify for the next round. He was devastated!

He dreaded going home to face the proverbial family choir singing songs of hollow sympathy. What he did not need at that moment was their less-than-supportive problem-solving sermons. Overwhelmed, disappointed, and spinning mentally out of control, he continued to battle feelings of being a forever failure. He resolved not to give up and considered, "What's next?" He realized that every job he had so far in life required physical labor. Through enough trial and error, he concluded it was time to do the opposite. What mindset shift was needed to compensate for these failures? If the physical was not working, he mused, "Time to try something cerebral." He subsequently enrolled in a local community college with nothing to lose by taking courses in business. Given low expectations among a student body of 11,000, he would blend into the environment. "What's the worst thing that could happen?" he asked himself. Focused on his schoolwork, for the first time in his life, he scored good grades. This subsequently created a positive feedback loop and ultimately led him to earn an associate's degree.

COMPENSATION ON THE NEXT LEG OF HIS JOURNEY

Feeling better on the path to a bachelor's degree, Anthony enrolled in the Mercy College School of Business in the New York City suburbs. With high hopes and feeling better about the next phase of his education, he drove to campus for the first day of the rest of his life. But, when he walked onto campus, something felt off. His instincts were guarded. As Anthony looked around, he was uncomfortable in his own skin. He knew from experience what it felt like to not fit in. But not like this. His introverted personality was compounded by a factor he hadn't considered—he was five years older than his mates. They looked, dressed, and acted like eighteen-year-olds. He was one year older than most college graduates. Integrating life experience, a big age difference, and a bundle of insecurities, how was he going to compensate? He was on unfamiliar turf and surrounded by a student body he did not relate to. Most were living in the dorms, with a social life formed by well-established cliques. Where did he fit in? How to compensate for the void he felt every time he walked into class?

The only solace: There were no sit-ups to test his fitness and no cars that needed repair. At least in college he could keep his head down, attend class, and learn something. It was better than the alternative—an unfulfilling life in a humdrum job with no prospects for a fulfilling career. Could this finally offer what no other environment did? What kind of compensation was needed to move comfortably into this new phase?

Compensation

Noun

Psychology: a mechanism by which an individual attempts to make up for some real or
imagined deficiency of personality or behavior by developing or stressing another aspect
of the personality, or by substituting a different form of behavior.

In a summer high school program prior to starting his junior year at Mercy, Anthony was asked to speak to col-lege-bound seniors. Given his work experience and uncon-ventional college path, he offered a different perspective. Feeling trepidation that he "can't even make a toast at my family's dinner table," Anthony gave it a try. As terrify-ing as it was, he survived to live another day. Fortunately, a spark ignited and prompted him to consider possibilities he never contemplated. With a relatively small student body compared to the community college, maybe "Standing out was the right mindset, given the challenges of fitting in." However, he knew public speaking came with social judgment and proverbial land mines. "What if I make a mistake? What if I'm not perfect? Will it erode my self-esteem even more?" Anthony knew he had to work on his public speaking skills but set it aside as he started classes in accounting, finance, and economics. He eventually settled into the daily routine of school and was upbeat about the future.

This is where Anthony's most important moment comes to life. He learned from that day forward how to compensate for the unplanned and unexpected.

Given the small student body at the Mercy College School of Business, extracurricular activities offered opportunities for experiential learning to develop important career competencies. One organization heavily supported by colleges worldwide is called Enactus, an acronym for Entrepreneurial Action Us. They educate, inspire, and support students to use innovation and entrepreneurship to solve many of the world's biggest problems. Each college team brainstorms the creation of a new company to drive social change and organizes itself to mirror the structure of real companies. With C-suites, departments, and employees intent on serving the company's mission, it looks and feels like any company a student is likely to join after college.

Given Enactus' template for tournament participation, students work for several months to conceive and develop their ideas. Efforts culminate in a yearly competition that brings colleges together for this epic event. Teams have ten minutes to pitch their idea to a jury comprised of executives from the world's leading companies. Feeling like the television show *Shark Tank*, one college is selected as "National Champion." There are college bragging rights. And, quite possibly, a businessperson on the jury becomes so enthralled by a student, they may interview him or her afterward for consideration for a full-time job with their company after graduation.

Striving to prepare the team for this event, Anthony was selected by his peers to be the CEO. This was his first foray into a leadership role. Feeling a great sense of pride, he subsequently gathered everyone, thanked them for the opportunity, and gave thought to what this project would look like. Great expectations awaited. With a year-end event in Ohio, this was an opportunity to shine like no other! The short-term goals and objectives were straightforward. Coalesce on one big idea, bring it to life, and prepare the ten-minute pitch. Next stop—a giant convention center in downtown Cincinnati. Anthony was confident everyone on the team was as committed as he was, excited to see what this new project would bring.

Throughout weeks of executing the plan and synthesizing it into the pitch, they were off to a good start. With eight mates and a clear division of labor, they were thrilled to draft the presentation and enthusiastically headed to Ohio. Everyone knew their roles and understood what was needed to win the tournament. But...weekly meetings were a struggle. There were ups and downs with missed timelines and a few seemingly disengaged "employees." Things were not as seamless as planned. Although he had no precedence for this kind of collaboration, Anthony began to feel he was doing "most of the heavy lifting." Nonetheless, given his unwavering conviction, it was full steam ahead. A few days prior to the event, the pitch was drafted, edited, and ready to present. A few days later, the team boarded a plane, checked into the hotel, gathered around the dinner table, and established the game plan. "Tomorrow is the dress rehearsal. The following day is the pitch," they agreed.

Although I was on faculty at Mercy then and Anthony was my student, I was not part of the Enactus project. Aware of his involvement, I was glad he was CEO, and knew all his teammates. A few days before the tournament, their faculty advisor was unable to travel and asked me to accompany the team instead. Handing me the mentoring baton, he said, "Please help them refine the pitch. It needs a little work." Since most of them had me in a class that emphasized public speaking, I happily agreed. I enjoyed teaching Anthony and his mates and was delighted to play a part in this phenomenal active learning experience. The students were smart, affable, and coachable. They were excellent at taking feedback and improved their skills at every turn. This was going to be a pleasure!

While every team member had a hand in assembling the pitch, Anthony wrote more than half of it. His role was to draft the script based on an Enactus-provided rubric. The others contributed content specific to their task. He then integrated the material into one seamless PowerPoint deck.

There was flexibility on content but a uniform set of mandatory guidelines for the judges to compare to other presentations. Compulsory items included a mission statement, organizational chart, and financial statements. Following the presentation, judges tallied each piece, aggregated the scores, and submitted them to a centralized Enactus desk to compare to hundreds of other pitches. Given the round-robin structure, teams were either eliminated or advanced to the next round.

The night before the big event we practiced the pitch. Since this was the first time I had seen it, there was room for improvement. Nothing substantive. I made a few "You might want to add this, delete that" types of comments. I was careful not to intrude on what they worked hard for months to compile. I offered suggestions on style and tempo and a few things to fine-tune the content. I had a great working relationship with everyone including Anthony and saw blue skies ahead. Win or lose, they were excited, working diligently, and taking feedback well. Win or lose, it didn't matter to me. The experience was unlike any I had in college and was blessed to contribute to this wonderful project. As we practiced the night before, everyone was adjusting to the coaching with one exception...Anthony. Without expressing a word, his body language spoke volumes. I could sense he was unhappy with something or someone but didn't know what. As a teacher and father in these moments, I draw a fine line between whether to move in or back off, providing sufficient space to let them sort out their issues. If they ask for help, I'm happy to offer.

Consequently, I provided final presentation feedback, called it a night, and agreed to meet in the morning to finalize it. At breakfast, we would lock down the final pitch to present that afternoon to a jury with executives from Walmart, Home Depot, and Coca-Cola.

At breakfast, we had a few hours to finalize it all and ample time to make last-minute adjustments. But, from the opening, I noticed they were speaking significantly faster than the night before. The volume of information was overwhelming, presented at a rapid-fire pace. Key presentation points were lost in the speed. It was hard to keep up. They subsequently admitted after we called it quits the night before, they kept revising the script, adding more than they took away.

Now, in the "eleventh hour" the presentation was too long. Since exceeding the time limit was not an option, material had to be cut. While the speech content was taking a hit, so was Anthony's ego. He did not appreciate the parts being deleted. But I did not know who authored any part of it. I had no agenda other than to determine the best possible integration of content, speech tactics, and time. The mission was to "cut here, slow down, cut some more" until we reached the perfect equilibrium. However, to Anthony, this was personal. We were deleting material, unbeknownst to me, that he had worked so hard to complete. The source of his frustration was now clear with every comment.

Although he was upset and feeling vulnerable, I approached him in front of the team and said, "This project is not about you. We will pitch all this in one voice. We have a shared goal and nothing else matters. We all agree we're trying to find time to meet the rubric's objectives. You are coming across as selfish, protecting your turf, indifferent to the mission. You are serving only yourself. Please do not lose sight of the goal so we can make adjustments that benefit the team. I appreciate how hard you worked to bring this all to fruition. Your efforts are respected. But my suggestion: Help everyone ascend the mountain as one unit, despite the obstacles we're facing. Right now you have a choice. Put your lines back and risk the credibility and trust you have worked to develop since this project began. Or remove your ego to serve the greater good. You decide right now. Which is it?" This moment is best captured by Marcus Aurelius' underscoring a key leadership principle, "Whenever you are about to find fault with someone, ask yourself the following question: What fault of mine most nearly resembles the one I am about to criticize?"

Anthony fought back tears. For the first time in his life he was on the receiving end of something he needed to hear. At that moment it dawned on him. The honest, sincere feedback was not a burden designed to ruin his self-esteem but an opportunity to discover what it meant to lead. He realized that great leaders:

- Place team needs first.
- Make their mates shine.
- Support them at every turn.
- Inspire, persuade, and provoke change.
- Cede control and ownership as needed for the sake of the mission.

- Provide constructive feedback to drive individual and team performance.
- Speak with candor and sincerity.
- Recognize the importance of tradeoffs.
- Make sacrifices to ensure successful outcomes.

He had worked nights and weekends to get everything perfected for the presentation. His pride of ownership was absolute! As we took stock of the learning outcomes in that moment, I concluded with him, Anthony did not...

- Empathize with mates, pushing them too hard.
- Understand why he could not force greatness from his team.
- Collaborate effectively. His staunch "I did most of the heavy lifting" was on display, causing conflict with no experience by which to solve it.

For what may have felt like the first time in his life, Anthony was not being judged. Although a bitter pill to swallow, he embraced the tough love and saw the light. He had a challenging history dating back to grade school when others made him feel inadequate. Feedback hurt, often delivered in a manner made to feel personal. "You should do this." "If only you had done that." From that moment on, it was a stunning realization of what it meant to lead. Any criticism offered was meant to be constructive, to further a mission bigger than himself.

Anthony took time at that moment to step away, sit down, and reflect on the advice offered. I appreciate how communication can feel devastating and destructive. However, this is where the growth occurs—in the discomfort or those revealing moments that develop the best versions of ourselves. It is a learned behavior. Some people may be predisposed to qualities we associate with leadership, but it takes commitment, education, and lessons born from mistakes to be effective. Learning the hard way, while stressful, is the most impactful. People remember the specific moments that became their catalyst for change.

Anthony carried these leadership lessons forward and never lost sight of what it means to lead. These became his foundation for career success, most notably climbing up the ranks at Google. Until he interviewed in Silicon Valley with this phenomenal organization, he had never been west of the Mississippi River. Who could have predicted this arc would lead him to Google?

Through the years, Anthony learned invaluable lessons that changed the course of his life. By putting ego aside and listening effectively, he began to understand the importance of leadership communication. Having come to this project from a base that had not exposed him to these outcomes, he realized that being Emotionally Intelligent redefined what it means to be smart. His moment sparked the introspection that inspired him to work on overcoming his introverted nature. The continued failures he felt growing up further compounded his desire to remain introverted. Yet, he acknowledged this weakness and strove to improve it. To sustain the capacity from repairing cars to managing compensation strategy at one of the world's greatest companies is a story for the ages.

That moment at Enactus set Anthony on a path of self-change that enabled him to be successful in every stage of his career climb. He also shared that he developed a much greater sense of intuition. Being better in touch with himself improved his capacity to read others. Each lesson he learned from failure culminated in astounding success.

That "moment" hit Anthony like a lightning bolt. As a direct consequence, it shocked him to do a complete 180-degree mindset turn—from selfishly wanting control and credit to always ensuring that others are recognized even if his work goes entirely unnoticed. I saw firsthand how the adoption of this philosophy and attitude propelled him not just in his career but in life. While his peers love collaborating with him, Anthony found massive fulfillment in his transformation to be far more important than any promotion, money, or reward.

When that lightning struck, he saw a vision of what great leadership looked like and plotted a course to become the change he wanted to be in the world. He then thoughtfully and methodically changed his behaviors to become a leader others admire and choose to follow. In the words of Carl Jung, "I am not what happened to me, I am what I choose to become." As he heightens the contrast between two extreme leadership styles, Anthony reminds himself daily of the power and importance his behavioral development had to impact others beyond his wildest dreams. With great enthusiasm and conviction, Anthony now views personal and professional matters rooted in the integration of Stoicism and Emotional Intelligence.

Self-Awareness	Self-Management	Social Awareness	Relationship Management
Assessment	Self-Control	Empathy	Conflict Management
Confidence	Transparency	Service to Others	Collaboration
	Adaptability		Influence

SIGNIFICANT DEVELOPMENT IN ALL FOUR EQ DIMENSIONS

Self-Awareness: Anthony lacked confidence as he transitioned into his new world, constantly hounding himself with thoughts of failure. He lacked awareness of his emotional state, unable to recognize how his behavior impacted others. He was trying so hard not to fail; he ignored any emotional signals needed to succeed. Surrounded by people who expected him to fail further exasperated his coping mechanism to defend himself and reveal his blind spots.

Self-Management: Anthony learned to keep disruptive emotions in check. Each time he heard that voice in the back of his head calling him a failure, it chipped away at his self-confidence.

Social Awareness: Anthony was unable to read the room and pick up on others' emotions. He may have heard what others said, but in his quest to self-protect, he did not understand the dynamic needed to become a powerful and compelling leader.

Relationship Management: Anthony did not handle conflict effectively. His ego stood tall, defending any threat that may have diminished it. He was not sensitive to others' feelings and learned the tools of Emotional Intelligence to successfully manage future interactions.

Viewing his changes through a leadership lens, Anthony struggled in some way at each of the EQ quadrants. As part of his magnificent evolution, he now excels at all of them. The transformation is astonishing! How fascinating to see his evolution guide him into the profession of compensation analyst. Until that revelatory moment, he failed to compensate for his perceived shortcomings. He did not have impactful learning moments to spark his transformation. Since so many in his circle expected "another Anthony failure" his negative self-talk was his default. His failures were self-fulfilling prophecies. Once he saw the benefit of these critical leadership lessons, he started to think and see himself differently. As Marcus Aurelius addressed his troops, he encouraged them to "Dig within. Within is the wellspring of Good; and it is always ready to bubble up, if you just dig."

What is exceptional about Anthony's "moment" is how quickly he understood why and how to correct these imbalances. As Rolf Dobelli, an unwavering Aurelias fan, wrote in *The Art of the Good Life*, "We're very good at planning. But we underestimate the importance of self-correction." Anthony's gut punch caused him to compensate for what he previously had not learned. His planning was stellar. His ability to self-correct was not in his mindset. He has subsequently matured immensely and frequently regards Aurelius' advice,

"It is the responsibility of leadership to work intelligently with what is given, and not waste time fantasizing about a world of flawless people and perfect choices." And finally, Anthony learned from the Stoics about behavior, collaboration, and the importance of reinforcement, "If you have been placed in a position above others, are you automatically going to behave like a despot? Remember who you are and whom you govern—that they are kinsmen, brothers by nature, fellow descendants of Zeus."

Anthony has considered the nature of compensation since the day he left Cincinnati. From college to PepsiCo to Google, he recognized how pay comes in many forms. Whether a glass of beer, stock options, or fulfillment, he pays his family and Google every day. When I think of Anthony, I envision Marcus Aurelius in his tent, looking at Anthony, proclaiming, "To do only what is right, say only what is true, without holding back. What else could it be but to live life fully—to pay out goodness like the rings of a chain, without the slightest gap."

CALL TO ACTION

To Compensate

> "When you wake up in the morning, tell yourself: the people I deal with today will be meddling, ungrateful, arrogant, dishonest, jealous, and surly."

Marcus Aurelius

When the great general wrote that, did he apply it to everyone in his path? Or, was he having a bad day and lashing out at his egomaniacal colleagues who saw things through the lens of their self-interests? We will never know. However, I relate to those words of wisdom. It is a cautionary tale to prepare for human-made, unexpected roadblocks. He reinforced the notion, "Where there are people, there's conflict."

Although unpredictable, I have collaborated with many generous, top-notch professionals who make going to work a joy. On the other hand, I have had the displeasure of working with a few arrogant, self-absorbed, obnoxious people who spread their toxicity like fertilizer. While I left many of those meetings feeling tarnished, wondering, "What is wrong with people?" my coping mechanism was, "It's not personal." I used to think that way. Until I didn't.

I find working with those personality types to be corrosive and exhausting. To many of them, work is a zero-sum game. They may live their personal lives that way. I will never know. But I will not expand my relationship with them outside the office, in spite of any attempt for them to get better acquainted with me. In the few instances where there was an outreach, I discovered a hidden agenda. Many want a better position, more money, or, as I came to find out...my job! Not everyone will get what they want. Consequently, I see bitterness, jealousy, and dishonesty. Sadly, I've seen colleagues sabotage others' work. When discussing with one of my CEO clients which organizations he competes with, he changed the narrative and said with conviction, "I pay no attention to companies I compete with. Instead, I contend with people inside these walls. The enemy is within. Everyone in that C-suite wants my job and will go to any length to get it. Whether their behavior is covert or explicit, I am amazed at what people will do to get what they want."

To put this into context, I learned over eight years of executive coaching, notwithstanding more money, people want the three P's in their careers:

- Power (comes in many forms)
- Pride
- Prestige

These are noble goals that everyone should aspire to attain. I also agree some will go to any length to acquire them. I learned the hard way to be cautious, as their behavior can be destructive and a corporate culture cancer. It is hard enough dealing with them in the confines of a one-hour meeting every now and then, much less, working with them over many months or even years.

Meetings to them are competitions. They win, you lose. They want the three P's and will work diligently to ensure you don't get them. I have been abused, belittled, and put down. Some of my colleagues seem intent on picking a fight and will not leave that meeting until someone in their gravity feels small. It is a sad state of human affairs that we have to deal with these types. Fortunately, companies these days recognize that. For instance, Jamie Dimon, CEO of JP Morgan Chase, says when looking to recruit, the bank seeks three characteristics:

- Capability
- Character
- How you treat others

He even states, "To know a candidate, I don't have to meet them. I can call their colleagues, friends, and spouse to find out who they are." Kudos to Dimon for raising the bar on professional behavior. However, there is no avoiding the archetype I am describing. Sometimes you will see the proverbial wolf in sheep's clothing, which only reveals their true nature later. Other times, you meet the eight-hundred-pound gorilla, beating his chest, lashing out at colleagues trying to prove to the world how great they are. What to do? The answer is rooted in one word: *compensate*. But for what? Them, or us?

It is infuriating to take proverbial punches from people you neither like nor respect. I have had my share of arguments and acted like a complete jerk in one meeting five years into my career at Bloomberg. One colleague, whose life mission was to press my buttons, baited me. I fell into his trap and lashed out in front of everyone directing my anger at him. I lost control and was embarrassed and ashamed at my behavior. I should have known better. I let my guard down, learned a lesson, and went home that night asking myself, "How do I compensate for the bad will that lurks in the course of a regular workday?"

Given my ignorance then of the human capacity to self-regulate behavior, this was the origin of my Stoicism journey. I did not appreciate then how useful and impactful it would become and happily acknowledge the principles that are infused now in every aspect of my life. I admit back then I was only dabbling in the philosophy, looking for a quick fix to overcome my humiliation. I had a problem that needed to be solved. Blaming my colleague Tom for his atrocious behavior was no remedy. One day he would be gone, and another "Tom" would be in that same seat. I can neither change them nor predict when the next one will come along. Instead, I took responsibility and recognized that changing myself was the only cure.

Stoicism teaches us to take stock of every situation. When locked in an argument going nowhere but down, take a step back. Look at the circumstances and ask yourself, "Is this terrible or do I just think it is?" Try not to overthink these confrontations. You always have a choice: Stand and take it, walk away, or something in between? Fight, freeze, or flight. You make the call every time and can come out unscathed, knowing you took the higher ground.

Stoicism tips to compensate for others' behavior and your measured responses:

1. When pushed to the brink, stop talking, smile.

2. "Kill" them with kindness.

3. "Tom" is trying to provoke a reaction from you. If you must say something, do what Nikki Haley, former governor of South Carolina, says when pushed: "Bless your heart."

4. Assuming you stay silent (my best advice) your body language will speak volumes. Let it do the talking. I practice this with my clients all the time. Do not fold your arms in a defensive posture. Instead, activate positive body language. Lift your shoulders, put your hands in the steeple position. Hands are not concealed. Nothing is hidden. This shows you are transparent in your dealings and in control of your mind and body.

5. Keep it slow. No need to rush. Look at him and keep smiling. Let him talk.

6. When he finishes, ignore him. This will make him angry and likely keep him talking. The more the talks, the bigger hole he digs. As Will Rogers said,

"When you find yourself in a hole, stop digging." These bullies find it hard to stop talking.

7. Keep smiling and pretend "Tom" does not exist. He has not earned your respect to acknowledge his presence. This is tough to do, especially when dealing with a senior employee. Stay the course; do not fold.

8. If the meeting is still going, and you have nothing left to say, push your chair back a few inches from the table. Keep your hands in the steeple position and place them on your lap. This will show a calm and cool exterior—exactly what "Tom" does not want.

9. Leave the meeting. He does not exist. Go back to your desk, office, wherever you can clear your head. Consider what just happened. If you can, break out *Meditations* and get lost in it, if only for a while. It is hard to go back to business as usual when provoked like that.

10. Think about the lessons learned. Believe it or not, this gets easier with each instance.

With luck, the bully will stay away or direct his derision at someone else. Tough to predict—just treat it as a Stoic does. Dispassionately detached from that last interaction that inflicted the pain. Recognize the learning outcomes and the need to build on this exercise of self-conditioning.

CHAPTER 7

Uwe Dockhorn:
To Bridge

Noun

1. A structure carrying a road, path, or canal across a river or other obstacle.

2. The elevated, enclosed platform on a ship from which the captain and officers direct operations.

Verb

3. To reduce the differences that separate two things or groups.

Example: "This collection of stories bridges the gap between history and fiction."

At the age of twenty-eight, five years after his father's death, Uwe Dockhorn was standing on the edge of a bridge in southern Germany staring into the void below, a howling wind whipping all around him. Pitch black and bitter cold, he was preparing to let go of the railing and let go of his life.

Standing over the abyss, he leaned forward and asked himself, "Can I let go?" Instead of releasing the handrail and plunging into the freezing water below, he felt something inside. A feeling was inside him that he had not sensed for over a decade, a tiny spark of light. At that moment, it kept him from jumping. Through massive tears and a release unlike any he had ever experienced, Uwe awakened to the idea that there must be another way to live through his pain.

This metaphorical spark not only provided the strength to pull himself back from that bridge rail, but it also offered lessons he would carry for the rest of his life—Uwe's two-part mechanism for self-transformation: letting go and letting in.

His moment evokes the early stages of a flower budding from the ground in spring. Earlier in his life, a seed was planted, unbeknownst to Uwe, that germinated and grew into profound personal development and a life-altering evolution.

Given life's ups and downs, what drives a young man to contemplate suicide?

Sexual assault can happen to anyone, no matter your age, sexual orientation, or gender identity. According to the Independent Commissioner for Child Sexual Abuse Issues in Germany, "Two representative studies in recent years concluded that nearly every seventh...adult in Germany suffered sexual violence during their childhood and adolescence.... Many of these cases are not included in the crime statistics because they are never reported."[11]

Men and boys who have been sexually assaulted report many of the same feelings and reactions as other survivors. In many cases, they face additional challenges because of social attitudes and stereotypes about men. According to 1in6.org, common experiences shared by boys who survived sexual assault include:

- Anxiety, depression, and post-traumatic stress disorder.

- Withdrawal from relationships and/or an increased sense of isolation.

- Worry about disclosing the event for fear of judgment or disbelief.[12]

When Uwe was ten, he was sexually abused and subsequently buried his trauma deep inside. So emotionally distraught, "He couldn't talk to anyone about the incident." For the next eighteen years, he "felt nothing." Something was missing, but he had "no clue" what it was. As he grew up, Uwe overcompensated for the emptiness and was addicted to alcohol and drugs, striving to fill a void he could not define.

---

11   "Figures on Child Sexual Abuse in Germany." UBSKM. Accessed July 17, 2023. https://beauftragte-missbrauch.de/en/themen/definition/figures-on-child-sexual-abuse-in-germany.

12   "Sexual Abuse & Assault of Boys & Men: Confidential Support for Men." Sexual Abuse & Assault of Boys & Men | Confidential Support for Men, March 30, 2023. https://1in6.org/.

"I LOST EVERYTHING."

When Uwe stood on that bridge and experienced that powerful moment of clarity, truly feeling life again, the seed began to sprout! He described it as letting in a small spark that eventually grew into a powerful flame. Thus, the second half of Uwe's transformation equation was born. The first is a lesson in Stoicism. The second has roots in Emotional Intelligence by developing the empathy to feel others and "let them in."

> *Letting go and letting in—the two-part mechanism that was Uwe's equation for self-transformation.*

Uwe describes this revelation as "energy, positive thoughts, and a sense of certainty, letting go of self-doubt, negativity, and stress. And the more you do it, the more it happens. It's like a switch you can consciously flip to strengthen and re-energize."

This lesson played the role of a muse years later in his life, when at the age of forty-two, further clarity struck again! This lucidity changed the course of his career. After years of being coached, he finally understood who he was and what he was put on this planet to do. He decided to become a coach himself and help others grow by teaching them how to let go and let in.

In 2016, a moment occurred to shape and solidify his resolve. Six days before Christmas, Uwe's mother passed away and he lost the last remaining member of his core family. At that moment, the seed germinated, poked through the ground, and fully bloomed. Uwe consequently cemented his understanding of the importance of family.

His coaching practice thus evolved into serving not just his clients, but his clients' significant others too. Referred to as his VIPs, Very Important Partners, Uwe helps them grow personally...emphasizing how to better relate to their loved ones.

Before he engages a client, Uwe asks some profound questions to help them get in touch with their inner selves... and asks their partners to do the same.

If you or your spouse/significant other answers yes to any of these questions...

- Do you feel depressed and stressed out?
- Are you tired all the time?
- Do you have a negative outlook on life?
- Are you using shopping, pills, or food and drink to help you feel better?
- Do you feel lonely and disconnected from your spouse, family, and friends?

...then Uwe's expertise may be the remedy for what ails you and your partner.

In his view, the problem is simple. "The two of you do not get enough free time together to strengthen your relationship in key areas such as mutual support, respect, fun and relaxation, and love and intimacy." Ignoring these symptoms makes it worse and eventually leads to a complete relationship breakdown. He stresses that the situation can improve with a little commitment from both sides and dedicates his life in the service of helping to heal marriages and/or partnerships.

By not completing suicide on the bridge that day, what impact did Uwe have on the world by letting go and letting in?

According to Netzwerk Suizidprävention, every fifty-three minutes somebody in Germany takes his or her life. Every four minutes someone tries. There are more deaths through suicide than murder, traffic accidents, and drug abuse combined. They estimate that the number of attempts is ten times higher. According to Our World in Data, close to 700,000 people die globally from suicide yearly. That's one person every forty seconds, making it a leading cause of death worldwide. Suicide is more common than homicide in most countries—often as much as ten to twenty times higher. In the United States, suicide is the twelfth leading cause of death. In 2020, 45,979 died with an estimated 1.2 million attempts.[13]

Flash forward to 2023. Uwe is "The Lifestyle Liberator" for high achievers and their families and delivered more than 17,000 successful sessions for power couples all over the globe these past fourteen years. His approach is grounded on principles of time freedom, autonomy, equality, and inner certainty that yield results financially and emotionally.

---

13 Saloni Dattani, Lucas Rodés-Guirao, Hannah Ritchie, Max Roser, and Esteban Ortiz-Ospina (2023). "Suicides." OurWorldInData.org. https://ourworldindata.org/suicide.

NEGATIVES INTO POSITIVES:
THE STOIC PHILOSOPHY

What could have signified Uwe's end was instead the start of his metamorphosis. The choice to not give up was not made only in this moment, but continually in a story of resilience as he walked away from the edge of that bridge. Yet, it begs the question, if he had not felt numb for so many years, would he have acknowledged that tiny spark when he balanced his life on the precipice?

> *What if he did not have that moment of clarity or never endured the realization of letting go and letting in?*

By letting go and letting in, he started to practice it constantly, becoming stronger each time he worked through it. He intentionally developed his inner strength to further empower clients, helping them to "be in the moment, to feel and perceive the world around them" as they reconnect to the people who matter most.

Uwe embraced letting go of his ego—he stopped blaming and accepted responsibility for his actions which ties strikingly to his two-part mechanism. According to Phil Jackson, ultra-successful Chicago Bulls and Los Angeles Lakers basketball coach, "Letting go is a necessary, if sometimes heart-wrenching, gateway to genuine transformation."

Was Uwe's experience on the bridge good or bad? The Stoics believed that events are not inherently either, it's the mind that makes it so. While most things that happen are beyond our control, there is one thing we do control...our ability to judge the event.

- By releasing the handrail, Uwe exerted control in that moment and saw it as the turning point to lead a powerful transformation for himself.

- Virtue and vice are integral parts of Stoic ethics. They are connected to what they call "Living in accordance with nature." Virtue is divided into *wisdom, justice, courage, and moderation,* and vice into *foolishness, injustice, and cowardice.* According to the Stoics, vice always leads to misery and virtue to happiness. By flipping excessive drinking and drug abuse into a life of service, Uwe replaced the vices with the virtues by letting go of his self-destruction and letting in a world of endless possibilities, helping others to live loving and productive lives.

- As with Uwe's two-part mechanism, it feels like what the Stoics call the Dichotomy of Control. This principle is one of the most popular in this philosophy and easy to understand why. According to Epictetus, *"The chief task in life is simply this: to identify and separate matters so that I can say clearly to myself which are externals not under my control, and which have to do with the choices I actually control."*

By letting go, we shed ourselves of the enormous burden and expectations that become factors for unhappiness. By letting in, we open ourselves to all people, places, or events despite having no power to control the outcomes.

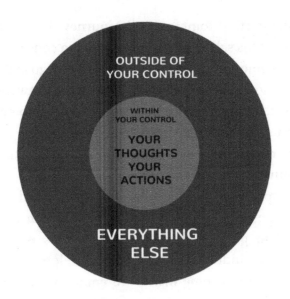

To underscore his premise, Epictetus said, "Within our power are opinion, aim, desire, aversion, and whatever affairs are our own. Beyond our power are body, property, reputation, office, and, in one word, whatever are not properly our own affairs."

UWE'S EMOTIONAL INTELLIGENCE DEVELOPMENT

Uwe speaks often and highly of the time needed to self-reflect, as he did not know who he was or his life's purpose. His self-reflection allowed the muses to speak to him and develop his transformative methods for personal change. Consequently, Self-Awareness ties beautifully to Uwe's evolution.

As the starting point for his EQ journey, those reflections empowered his self-regulation. Uwe had to consistently recognize his emotional state to know how to let go and what to let in. He now coaches the recognition of Self-Awareness to his clients, giving him the perspective needed to enlighten his clients on how to develop Self-Awareness in themselves, furthermore, how their behaviors impact their VIPs and families.

Uwe speaks of the discipline needed to implement his AIM—Experience program and when shifting behaviors, the need to practice them repeatedly. This is a strategy and tactic for individual and marital development that are the epitome of keeping disruptive emotions and impulses in check. These are not single events, but habits one must adopt, develop, and continually practice. He inspires others to commit to investing in themselves and the people who love them.

Self-Awareness	Self-Management	Social Awareness	Relationship Management
Assessment	Self-Control	Empathy	Conflict Management
Confidence	Transparency	Service to Others	Collaboration
	Adaptability		Influence

As a result of his Social Awareness development and life's reorientation to serve, Uwe is a prime example of

Relationship Management. This is no surprise, since he developed a distinct method to bring couples together in a world trying to constantly tear them apart. Uwe brings a sentiment to his practice that helps others recognize and believe that "The factors that bind us together are much stronger than any of the elements trying to pull us apart."

THE BRIDGES OF UWE'S LIFE

"Bridge the gap" is one of the most used idioms in English. It describes what is needed to connect ideas, spaces, and concepts. The expression is meant to connect two otherwise unrelated things by adding something or by finding common ground. When I consider Uwe's evolution, his unyielding dedication helping others help themselves is significant. Going to work each day in the service of strengthening marital bonds, coaching others to reconnect, and reminding them why they fell in love is joyful! When you review Uwe's website, he uses words like *power*, *results*, and *energizing*.[14] More important are the thought-provoking questions he asks clients, including, "Are you and your life partner struggling to find more intimacy, adventure, and connection?"

Uwe bridges the emotional gaps and examines where couples have been, where they are, and where they would like to go. In other words, he strives to accelerate the healing process with couples who have grown apart. Relying on him to bridge that gap, Uwe connects two people through his methods to make the differences between them minute

---

14   "Uwe Dockhorn: Liberating Lifestyles." Uwe Dockhorn | Liberating
      Lifestyles. Accessed July 17, 2023. https://www.uwedockhorn.com/.

and reclaim a partnership rooted in adoration, affection, and commitment.

To think that Uwe's moment happened on a cold blustery night, standing on a bridge, weighing the difference between life and death, who knew that is where his new story would begin? To help couples cross their proverbial bridge and reestablish a life built on a platform of love and lifelong devotion, is there any higher calling?

CALL TO ACTION

To Bridge

> *"We should not act when we are in the thralls of emotions, because we are likely to make mistakes, even when we are well intentioned."*
>
> Marcus Aurelius

According to McGill University in Montreal, Canada, the purpose of a bridge is "to allow people or cargo easy passage over an obstacle by providing a route that would otherwise be uneven or impossible."[15] In English, there are eleven idiomatic expressions with the word *bridge*, including:

- A bridge too far.

- To burn (one's) bridges.

- Cross that bridge when you get to it.

---

15   "Bridge." Accessed July 17, 2023. https://www.cs.mcgill.ca/~rwest/wikispeedia/wpcd/wp/b/Bridge.htm.

Perhaps the most relevant expression that ties disparate things together is to "bridge the gap" between two or more things. Such is the case when a bridge is built between Stoicism and Emotional Intelligence. The more I recognized the synergy, the more enlightened I became. When engaged in an interaction when I would formerly lose my temper, I learned to maintain my sense of control, give thought to what was happening, and respond with grace under the fire of anger and disdain.

To give credit to the great Stoics, my immediate mindset default in an interpersonal struggle became, "What would Marcus Aurelius say or do?" Through time, I built a catalog of insights and expressions integrating what I learned from these two subjects. They have become my best teachers and help me with interactions every day of my life. It took time and patience, built on a starting point in the 1990s that brings me to 2023. I commit to spending the rest of my life refining the bullseye between Stoicism and Emotional Intelligence.

Where to begin? The Stoics had a concept somewhat like Emotional Intelligence, the potential for humans to regulate emotional responses both to the outside world and with their inner voice. Stoicism also promotes empathy and understanding in our interpersonal relationships. Of chief importance is the ability to listen to others in a way that acknowledges their own values, beliefs, and autonomy.

However, this is where Stoicism is sometimes misunderstood: The goal of Stoic thought is not to minimize negative feelings but to cultivate virtue. To do the right thing all the time. Emotional Intelligence does not examine the concept of virtue achievement. Nor does it take a philosophical approach. However, it does address the emotional, personal, social, and survival dimensions of intelligence. Known as one of the career quotients, these Q's have been evolving among social scientists for years. They are gradually being included in company learning and development programs and are given enormous weight as critical leadership competencies.

Career Quotients	Q
Emotional	EQ
Creativity	CQ
Adaptability	AQ
Execution	XQ
Communications	CCQ
Cultural	CQQ
Positivity	PQ

Regarding Emotional Intelligence, it starts with identifying the biggest threat to people's success, which usually has little to do with technical competence, but more often than not, with mismanaging emotional triggers. The third piece of Jamie Dimon's JP Morgan Chase recruiting frame is "How you treat others."

This is where ancient Stoicism and modern Emotional Intelligence development intersect. In the workplace, space is available to acknowledge the full range of human emotional experiences as relevant. Since we are not robots, no one is ever asked to leave their emotions at home when they start a new job. Consequently, every emotion ever expressed at home is likely to play out at work in some form. Not as often nor with the same intensity, but it would be near impossible to ask a human not to bring their humanity to the workplace.

We laugh, cry, and celebrate things at work...not in the same way as with our spouses and children. But we recognize the range of emotions when we see them and tacitly agree on the boundaries that keep a workplace professional. Effective leaders hence strive to enact strategies and tactics to foster a healthy Emotional Intelligent culture as they realize the significant benefits. Seen a different way, they know the consequence of a corporate culture lacking in EQ. Imagine what your office would feel like if you could diminish (maybe never eliminate) all the pettiness and judgment that are associated with peoples' ill-tempered emotions and behavior.

EQ Competencies	Stoicism Cardinal Virtues	Shared Leadership Outcomes
Self-Awareness	Wisdom	Adaptability
Self-Management	Justice	Emotional Regulation
Social Awareness	Courage	Empathy
Relationship Management	Temperance	Conflict Resolution

Tools to Use to Integrate Stoicism and Emotional Intelligence

While There Are Many, Start with These Top Three:

"Practice really hearing what people say. Do your best to get inside their minds."

Marcus Aurelius

1. **Slow Your Emotional Reactions:** We make first impressions in 250 milliseconds. It is not intentional and took years of evolution. Behind the force of those impressions are our emotions. When you meet someone or are in a discussion that could potentially be inflammatory, be conscious of your intention to fight whatever impulse you feel, and count to three (you've seen this in other chapters—let's reinforce it). Hold this up to some self-scrutiny as your brain slows down and becomes more methodical before you speak. You will find over time it keeps you from blurting out the first thing that comes to mind and prevents embarrassment along the way.

2. **Practice Tactical Listening:** Active listening is hard work. It demonstrates empathy and shows a sincere desire to better understand what the other side is experiencing. Listening is a martial art, balancing the subtle behaviors of Emotional Intelligence and the assertive skills of influence to gain access to others' minds. Listening is never passive. It is the

most active thing you do. When someone is speaking, resist the impulse to interject or interrupt. Let them talk as much as needed. It will test your patience, but it is worth it to gain the respect and courtesy of others reciprocating by listening back as intently. It was Epictetus who said, "We have two ears and one mouth so we can listen twice as much as we speak."

3. **Lead Your Life:** As Seneca says, "Real power is to be in your own power." Although EQ had not yet been invented, Seneca was likely referring to what some of my clients consider their most important measurable competency: Self-Awareness. Regardless of their position, gender, or marital status, it does not matter. It is one thing to lead others, and quite another to lead yourself. A key tenet of this book is to know what you value, and make decisions inside your circle of dignity. That's easier said than done. Take time often to reflect on what is important, and do your best to drown out what is not. The more you work through that filter, the more instinctive you become on how to face adversity. You will find that the quality of your interactions increases your capacity to understand how to lead others.

CHAPTER 8

Dominic DiMaria:
To Matter

Noun

1. Physical substance in general, as distinct from mind and spirit.

2. An affair or situation under consideration.

Verb

1. Be of importance; have significance.

Soul

Noun

1. The spiritual or immaterial part of a human being or animal, regarded as immortal.

2. Emotional or intellectual energy or intensity, especially as revealed in a work of art or an artistic performance.

Forty-five thousand and five hundred years ago, on the Indonesian island of Sulawesi, someone entered a cave, faced the wall, picked up a brush, and sketched a pig, complete with back bristles and facial warts. In a study published in *Science Advances* in January 2021, an image shows the animal looking at two other pigs. Outlines of human hands are positioned near the swine's backside, with a small patch hinting at the possibility of a fourth creature.

The painting, created with strokes of ochre, a mineral made of silica and clay, was discovered in 2017 by archaeologists at Australia's Griffith University. According to Adam Brumm, an author of the study, "Cave paintings and related forms of artistic expression were most likely part of the cultural traditions of the first modern humans to spread out of Africa and into Asia and Australia." As far as they could ascertain, the paper says, "We are confident dating of the Sulawesi boar at Leang Tedongnge now seems to make it the oldest depiction of an animal that exists in the world. In addition, this dated image of a pig may also constitute the oldest known work of figurative art." According to *National Geographic*, "Such early glimmers of art reflect a vital shift in the way our ancestors engaged with their environment and the surrounding landscape," says April Nowell, a paleolithic archaeologist at the University of Victoria in British Columbia, "They're imbuing their place with meaning, significance, and symbolic dimension."[16]

---

16   Wei-Haas, Maya. "This 45,500-year-old Pig Painting Is the World's Oldest Animal Art." National Geographic. January 13, 2021. https://www.national geographic.com/science/article/45500-year-old-pig-painting-worlds-oldest-animal-art.

HOW DO WE KNOW THE CAVE PAINTING IS ART?

According to Philosophy Now, "Art is an expression of our thoughts, emotions, intuitions, and desires, but it is even more personal than that: it's about sharing the way we experience the world, which for many is an extension of personality. It is the communication of intimate concepts that cannot be faithfully portrayed by words alone. And because words alone are not enough, we must find some other vehicle to carry our intent. Art is to be found in how the media is used, the way in which the content is expressed."[17]

While historians cannot say with certainty when and where art started, these ancient paintings show us that even cavemen and women wanted to show us a snippet of how they lived. Additional age-old evidence of artistic behavior is human body decoration, including skin coloring and beads. Many ancient cultures also believed in tattooing as a form of body art. To our good fortune, art makes us think, laugh, and cry. It subsequently bridges the gap between cultures, languages, and time. Best of all, art helps us see things differently and brings fresh perspectives into our lives.

Creating art is one element of what it means to be human. When different professions debate why our species is distinct, you often hear priests, prophets, and philosophers communicate it is our "soul" that makes us unique. References to this potent word include, "She is the heart and soul of our team." Billy Joel sang passionately in one of his

---

17 "What Is Art? and/or What Is Beauty?" Philosophy Now. https:// philosophynow.org/issues/108/What_is_Art_and_or_What_is_Beauty.

THE MOMENT THAT DEFINES YOUR LIFE

hit singles, "It's all about soul." And as articulated in neuroscientist Antonio Damasio's superb book *Descartes' Error*, "Feelings form the base for what humans have described for millennia as the...soul."

According to the late, great Bruce Lee, "An artist's expression is his soul made apparent. Behind every motion, the music of his soul is made visible." Lee, who died in 1973 at the ripe young age of thirty-two, was a martial artist, actor, and philosopher. He was the founder of Jeet Kune Do, a hybrid martial arts philosophy drawing from different combat disciplines credited with paving the way for modern mixed martial arts (MMA). He is considered by many critics to be the most influential martial artist of all time, and a pop culture icon of the twentieth century who bridged the gap between East and West.

The philosopher in Lee left us a legacy best understood by how he regarded the integration of art and soul:

- "The ultimate aim of the artist is to lay hold of the art of living. Be a master of living, for the soul creates everything."

- "Creation in art is the psychic unfolding of the personality. Its effect is a deepening of the personal dimension of the soul."

When you learn about the life of this extraordinary man, he inspired a generation of artists to consider, "The aim of art is not the one-sided promotion of spirit, soul, and senses, but the opening of all human capacities—thought, feeling, will—to the life rhythm of the world of nature."

Dominic DiMaria is a multi-faceted, fervent creator and founder of a company fittingly called Soulmatter. Sharing Lee's ethos, he potently combines art, soul, and what matters to live a productive life in his work. He is staunch in his conviction that he does not solve problems through his art. On the contrary, his mission is to integrate the best of art and soul and "create problems, start a fire," and ignite the artistry that lives within you.

Dominic's transformation moment was sparked by a traumatic event several years ago. In the summer of 2015, he was high on life. He enjoyed his job, was putting money in the bank, and preparing a move to Los Angeles to advance his artistic aspirations. One fateful day, he was working late at the office, socializing with new employees about to start a six-week training program. Looking forward to meeting his brother Geno for dinner, Dominic hopped on his bicycle and rode through the streets en route to the restaurant. Suddenly, a Toyota 4Runner coming head-on took an unexpected left turn. Before Dominic could acknowledge what was happening, he smashed into the front side of the SUV. On impact, he broke his nose, shattered all his front teeth, and fractured his skull. When the EMTs arrived, they quickly slid him into the ambulance and rushed him to the hospital for emergency surgery.

Surviving the operation proved to be the easy part. It was the postsurgical trauma that weighed on him most. Dominic describes the early stages of anger and frustration stemming from the realization that "you can be doing everything right, full of love and life, and it can be indiscriminately taken away in the blink of an eye." In Dominic's postoperative experience, frustration became the driving emotion. Medical malpractice, bankruptcy, and a hospital indifferent to the suffering of its victims pushed him to the brink of despair. Sadly, darkness soon overtook what was once a sunny disposition. After moving back in with his parents and sleeping in his childhood bedroom, he continued to slide into a gloomier state of mind. Thoughts of self-harm began to bubble up from nowhere. Mindful he had no access to weapons, he started to seek alternatives. The journalist Sally Brampton called depression a landscape that "is cold and black and empty. It is more terrifying and more horrible than anywhere I have been, even in my nightmares."

Commuting two hours per day in his car, these periods of solitude became the canvas for his destructive thoughts. His only method of coping was to find an outlet for the distress painfully trapped inside. Driving the same dull highway each workday, Dominic developed a contaminated relationship with the rumble strips on the roadsides. Although it is a device invented to save lives, they began to test Dominic's mental fortitude. Urges to rip the wheel in one direction and send the car hurling into a ditch flashed through his mind. He was playing chicken with the rumble strips, building enough courage to cross them and collide with anything in his car's path. Day after day, he heard the thumping sounds of those strips under the tires, visualizing the crash that would end his life. With each ride, he tested fate, getting more comfortable with the idea of completing the suicide. As Mike Gerson, a *Washington Post* columnist, explained, "Depression is a malfunction of the instrument we use to determine reality." With no mental compass to guide him amidst a warped sense of reality, the immense weight of his anguish continued to seek an avenue for his final exit.

Then one evening, he tempted fate again. Crossing the rumble strip, he slanted quickly...and realized he needed help before he hurt himself so badly there would be no recovery. Dominic's need to live overruled his drive to die. Vulnerable, broken, and desperate, Dominic met with a religious counselor. He spilled his proverbial guts for more than one hour and was abruptly told, "Stop masturbating. Purify your mind, and the suicidal thoughts will go away." Beyond disgusted, he stormed out and vowed never to return.

His soul had been shattered long before, the hidden byproduct of that crash. Driving into that ditch splintered them further. Yet, the simple words of the counselor gave no relief. He had no sense of direction on which way to turn, having found his left swing into the ditch left him aching, and his right toward counseling did as well. Thus he spent the next two years fighting to keep himself above the thoughts weighing him down into the abyss of depression that had already captured him once before.

Getting treatment, finding the courage to look deep within, and embracing the idea of vulnerability was "worse than a gut punch." His mind was a bundle of confusion, back to rock bottom, mentally, emotionally, and spiritually. Landing there for what he hoped was the last time, Dominic sought alternative paths to deal with the pain. Unbeknownst to him, he was about to experience the moment that defined the rest of his life.

Candra James was the angel who appeared when Dominic needed it most. The initial therapy session was the exact opposite of his prior experience. As he shared his story with her, she replied, "I need you to know that what you're going through is an extreme experience, and your responses are normal. That is what happens, and I am glad you're here. Where would you like to begin?"

Candra validated Dominic's feelings. She listened intently and helped him understand why he was judging himself heavily and why suicide seemed so tempting. At that moment, she saved Dominic's life. Candra provided the perspective and support needed to allow the healing to enter his being. Like good artists who prompt others to change their outlooks, the Stoic philosophy supported her counseling with the premise that your life can only be as free as your perception of it. Whenever we look at a situation, we see our past in it, because every event gets interpreted, and interpretations are rooted in the past. Despite the horrific memories that came with the accident, Dominic was encouraged to see the circumstances differently. They were over and done. He was learning to interpret the accident from another vantage point. And, for the first time in months, he felt hopeful.

Prior to Candra coming into his life, Dominic was deeply disoriented with his internal battles, striving to build a mental fortress as his torment bore down on him, trying to put the pieces of his life back together again. He struggled to accept what happened and how to get through it. Caught in a proverbial trap with no escape, acceptance was an impossible reality. Every day, he felt the injustice of the situation weigh heavily on his soul. But, with Candra, the healing began. Without projecting moral judgment, she helped Dominic turn the corner and envision a future free of trauma and turmoil.

Every meeting brought Dominic closer to restoring the good health he worked so diligently to attain. He finally accepted the reality of these circumstances and allowed himself to release the pain and frustration so tightly held. This coincided with the conclusion of legal skirmishes fought to bring compensation from the accident. Once settled, Dominic sold his belongings, paid his debts, packed the car, and moved to Los Angeles to pursue his dream—to live a fulfilling life integrating his art and soul, committed to working on things that mattered. In other words, he used this as an opportunity to create Soulmatter. His artwork takes many forms and spans the gamut from film directing, screenwriting, and even sneaker creation. He explores multimedia, creating a variety of art that expresses his thoughts, emotions, and desires.

In *The End of Your World: Uncensored Straight Talk on the Nature of Enlightenment*, Adyashanti writes, "There's a phenomenon happening in the world today. More people are waking up—having real, authentic glimpses of reality. By this I mean that people seem to be having moments where they awaken out of their familiar senses of self...into a much greater reality...far beyond anything they knew existed." The author of this insightful book explains that for some, the awakening happens over time, while for others it happens in a moment, perhaps even a split second. "But in that instant, the whole sense of 'self' disappears. The way they perceive the world suddenly changes, and they find themselves without any sense of separation between themselves and the rest of the world. It can be likened to the experience of waking up from a dream—a dream you didn't even know you were in until you were jolted out of it."[18]

Candra helped Dominic awake from that nightmare. Through a confluence of events that put him on a downward spiral, his world collapsed. He lost his sense of self, leading to an existential crisis. He often considered driving off the roadside directly into the abyss. But, at that moment of revival, he realized with astonishing clarity that he was not limited by what he was working through. Like the great artist he is, he shifted his mindset to a healthy attitude that recognized "the unknown is just another term for creation." His soul experienced the material world through the lens of a newfound perception.

Drawing on lessons from the Stoics, Dominic describes that dismal moment with Candra, "I feel like my life ended that day because I was a different person on the other side of the experience." Once he "learned" to accept the past, he allowed himself to be present and sustain healthy moments throughout each day. He no longer self-identified as "Dominic, the man who was hit by a truck and had his life ruined." He was now "Dominic, the Artist in Chief." With a

---

18   Adyashanti. *The End of Your World: Uncensored Straight Talk on the Nature of Enlightenment.* Boulder, CO: Sounds True, 2010.

renewed sense of purpose, his art started to light proverbial fires, igniting the passion he discovered that lived inside him all along. With a freshly healed soul, he never glanced into that rearview mirror again. His eyes were focused one way—straight ahead!

Dominic would have made even the most ardent Stoics proud by finding the courage to let go of the trauma-induced identity. The torment of having his life stripped in a moment by something entirely out of his control is hard to fathom. The courage to say, "I don't identify with this trauma. I identify with being a healed person," was poignant. As Dominic developed his spiritual fortress, he likely heard the Stoics whispering, "You have power of your mind—not outside events. Realize this, and you will find strength." Dominic's continued maintenance of mental health was integral to sustaining his well-being.

LEARNING TO BE EMOTIONALLY INTELLIGENT

From that moment, Dominic changed his perspective. He describes it through the lens of emotional strengthening and maintenance: rebuilding a foundation of mental health, identifying and unlearning damaging behaviors, releasing the victim mindset, embracing vulnerability, and

practicing habits of empowerment. This became the framework by which he created his newfound healing practices to restore the mind, heart, and soul.

Consequently, on the Self-Awareness spectrum, he traveled from one end to the other, and acknowledged the need for help, given his bleak mental state. After his emotional

well-being began to diminish, he lost any shred of mindful-
ness and the tools needed to climb out of the fog. His quiet
time commuting to and from work may just as well have
been a runaway train heading toward an immovable object.
There would be no collision that day, only the shifting perspective that led him to realize the signs were pointing him
in another direction.

For Self-Management, the entire series of events shined
a spotlight to keep his disruptive emotions and impulses in
check. Given recurrent suicidal tendencies, he persisted in
the pursuit of goals and opportunities, despite obstacles and
setbacks. This part of the EQ tool kit helped him see the light
at the end of the proverbial tunnel. Soon enough, the therapy led him to light fires, using his artistic skills as an integral
part of the recovery. His soul matter, the spirit buried deep
within, waiting to resurface, became his guidepost. He now
set foot on the ground he scantly recognized, a road to recovery and renewal.

Self-Awareness	Self-Management	Social Awareness	Relationship Management
Assessment	Self-Control	Empathy	Conflict Management
Confidence	Transparency	Service to Others	Collaboration
	Adaptability		Influence

Two foundational elements of Self-Management that
live in the regulation quadrant of Emotional Intelligence are
transparency and adaptability. Locked in his two-hour commute, Dominic's feelings of despair lacked both. Not sharing

what brewed inside, depression festered with no relief valve. Bottled up with a grip that tightened each day, listening to the tires collide with the rumble strips only exacerbated the symptoms. With no means to adapt, he continued to feel the pain as his senses were overwhelmed with suicidal sensations and only one way to alleviate them. Dominic's moment helped him to find an alternative path and recognize the value of his life was greater than the alternative.

As I became better acquainted with Dominic, he shared his education on the path to producing and directing movies. He believed the best way to learn filmmaking "was to make films." While classroom education and textbooks have their place to teach the technical aspects, nothing compares to lessons learned when creative and motivated people unify their efforts to support a common goal. As stated in one of my favorite books, *Yes And: Lessons from The Second City*, he shares their sentiment, "All of us is better than any one of us."

With an abundance of artistic talent, Dominic continually demonstrates the capacity to create and manage a wide variety of projects that begin with a blank slate. As I came to appreciate his cinematic flair, we often spoke of movie genres that impact us the most. Given we share a love of Steven Spielberg, three that came to mind in our assessment of his best works included *Band of Brothers*, *Schindler's List*, and *Saving Private Ryan*. They integrate masterful storytelling, innovative cinematic techniques, and lessons so unbearable one can only hope that countries will think twice before they engage an enemy in warfare.

When you watch this type of scene, the camera often pans to a lone soldier as the film strives to highlight the character's development. Hero or villain, story arcs evolve based on how they relate to the world around them. Whether it is people, places, or events, these movies tend to agree on one premise unbending in the mind of a warrior. While the American soldier's creed is to "place the mission first" there is another powerful sentiment every fighter knows when heading into battle. Their job is to protect their comrade to the right and protect their comrade to the left. With no energy needed to shield themselves, there is comfort in knowing that two fellow soldiers are always looking out for them. "I have your back, front, and flanks." The guardians are never far away, juxtaposed on either side, striving to defend their band of brothers and sisters from imminent enemy threats.

What happens then, when on a bicycle, cruising at thirty miles per hour with no one to support your sides? Or when driving solo at twice the speed, isolated and unprotected by a clear and present danger? On his bike during that moment, and on his daily car commute, Dominic lacked a safeguard. All he had were his faculties, the mental fortress whose limits would be tested at any moment. On a quest to heal the soul, he understood what Caroline Myss, author of *Invisible Acts of Power*, said, "The soul always knows what to do to heal itself. The challenge is to silence the mind."

A jumble of anguish and confusion, Dominic was a soldier, fighting to find peace, wondering whether he was going to ignite his fires or extinguish them once and for all. By silencing the mind in therapy, he developed the tools Candra empathetically offered. She had his front, back, and flanks. Art became the catalyst to reclaim his existence as he inspired his mates to gather around the proverbial campfires and share their stories.

After five years, Soulmatter evolved into an operating system, a way of being. He started to use the "don't solve problems" approach to develop the experiential fine art brand dasaüdie, the boutique sport fashion project TRASHGOD, and the premiere film label DeluxeVersion. Now, often in the edit bay bringing a film to fruition, his commitment to choose life is unwavering. He strives daily to contribute art that has meaning, significance, and prompts changes in perspective. Integrating tools of Stoicism and Emotional Intelligence on his road to recovery, Dominic internalized and acted on advice offered by Rumi, the thirteenth-century Persian poet, "There is a candle in your heart ready to be kindles. There is a void in your soul ready to be filled. Invite him to fill you up. Embrace the fire."

Soul
Matter

"My soul is not for sale."
"Eyes are the windows to your soul."
"Serena is your soul sister."

Aretha Franklin was an American singer, songwriter, and musician. According to Britannica, with over 75 million records sold globally, she is one of the world's bestselling artists.[19] She received numerous honors throughout her career and was even awarded the Presidential Medal of Freedom.

19 "Aretha Franklin." Encyclopædia Britannica. Accessed July 3, 2023. https://www.britannica.com/biography/Aretha-Franklin.

Born in Tennessee and raised in Detroit, Michigan, Aretha started singing professionally at twelve, occasionally traveling with the Soul Stirrers, an American gospel music group.

While her long and distinguished career twisted and turned to great heights, one of her extraordinary milestones occurred on January 20, 2009, when she sang "My Country, 'Tis of Thee" at President Barack Obama's inaugural ceremony. According to Richie Unterberger, a music journalist who followed Aretha's ascent, Franklin was "one of the giants of soul music, and indeed of American pop as a whole. More than any other performer, she epitomized soul at its most gospel charged. She has often been described as a great singer and musician due to vocal flexibility, interpretive intelligence, skillful piano-playing, her ear, and experience."

On the origins of soul music, this genre originated in the African American community throughout the United States in the late 1950s. It has roots in gospel music and rhythm and blues, according to The Telegraph. Some credit Ray Charles, the blind pianist nicknamed "The Genius," for "almost single-handedly" inventing it. Following Ray on that path, Aretha subsequently came to be known as the "Queen of Soul," with Sam Cooke as its king. With roots in gospel music and the broader Black church culture, soul music captured the spirit, emotions, and chaos of the 1960s civil unrest that continued into the next decade.

Since the soul sound took shape, the beginning of the modern Civil Rights movement became associated with songs that supported it. Ask people why they listen to it, and I often hear, "Because it is easy and accessible to listen to, it tugs at our emotional heartstrings, and taps into our sense of self like no other artform." In other words, it soothes the soul. Of the many reasons why people listen to music, one of them is clear: It is therapeutic. While formal therapy is the clinical use of music to accomplish individualized goals, such as stress reduction, many do without that formality to accomplish the same objective.

Since antiquity, there have been references in literature and ancient philosophy to music therapy. Stoicism, a school of thought to keep emotions calm given the disorder that exists all around, sheds light on this as it connects to music in unexpected ways.

WHERE MUSIC PLAYS A PART
FOR STOICS TO NOURISH THE SOUL

Melinda Latour is a historical musicologist and Assistant Professor at Tufts University. With an interest in many musical genres, she did extensive research on practices inspired by the revival of Stoicism in seventeenth-century France. Referred to by historians as Neostoicism, she discusses a fascinating piece of that movement in an article from *The Conversation* published in August 2022, "How Stoicism influenced music from the French Renaissance to Pink Floyd."[20]

"Emerging in the wake of the violent French Wars of Religion, Neostoics looked to Stoicism as a remedy for social

20   Latour, Melinda. "How Stoicism Influenced Music from the French Renaissance to Pink Floyd." The Conversation. August 16, 2022. https://theconversation.com/how-stoicism-influenced-music-from-the-french-renaissance-to-pink-floyd-181701.

and political instability. They developed a vocal music repertoire to teach the principles of the system, guiding singers and listeners to 'rehearse' Stoic techniques of emotional regulation through informal musical gatherings in people's homes."[21]

Combining two kinds of art, their songs illustrated, "Stoic principles through musical 'text painting,' in which specific words, actions or concepts were musically conveyed through sound—and, sometimes, visuals—in the score." For example, she notes a 1582 poem "L'eau va viste" by Antoine de Chandieu that was set to music evoking the sounds, sights, and feel of the wind as water gently flows, emitting a soothing, joyful experience. She notes, "Numerous Stoic writings, such as Seneca's *On the Brevity of Life*, evoke similar imagery of running water to warn against placing one's happiness in external comforts, which, like a current, quickly pass."

Flash forward to the 1970s. Latour demonstrates how Pink Floyd strikes a "similar musical reflection in their iconic song 'Time' from their 1973 album *Dark Side of the Moon*. The album outlines all the major forces and concerns that can drive people insane: aging, death, fear, greed, and violence." According to Roger Waters, one of the band's composers, the album is about "life with a heartbeat." The track opens with a meandering two-and-a-half-minute instrumental introduction, slowly building from a breathy synthesizer drone to the disorienting sound of numerous ticking clocks. Then there's a cacophony of alarms before listeners hear a mechanical

21   "The Gordon Collection and the French Wars of Religion." University of Virginia Library. https://explore.lib.virginia.edu/exhibits/show/renaissance-in-print/frenchwarsofreligion.

bass click that sounds like a metronome or a mechanical heartbeat.

"This unusual extended instrumental introduction desta-bilizes a listener's expectation of musical time and demands greater attention to the moment-by-moment sensations of its passing. The lyrics throughout the song reinforce this initial musical warning—that listeners must pay close attention to the flow of time and make sure it's used with purpose and meaning. 'The time is gone. The song is over,' the lyrics con-clude, 'Thought I'd something more to say.'"[22]

Latour asserts, "These two musical examples, composed nearly 400 years apart, model a core element of Stoic ther-apy: By meditating on the fragility of time, Stoics seek not to instill dread, but to reveal death and transience as natural aspects of the human experience that can be faced without anxiety. This calm acceptance offers a release from destruc-tive emotions like fear and yearning that pull our attention to the future and the past."

To heed Marcus Aurelius' advice, "Give yourself a gift—the present moment."

Latour then concludes that, "Stoicism and its abundant artistic echoes are easily misread as pessimistic because of this relentless focus on human mortality and fragility. This negative reading misses Stoicism's profoundly optimistic and empowering message, which is that our mental freedom remains in our control, regardless of external circumstances.

Consequently, if you find yourself upset, confused, or otherwise befuddled by life's circumstances, reading

---

22 Latour, "How Stoicism Influenced Music from the French Renaissance to Pink Floyd."

Meditations is one way to calm the nerves and bring order to a chaotic mind. However, given the human need for variety in all things, there are other outlets the Stoics turn to, as Latour says, "to thoughtfully unite words and sounds—and transform helpful Stoic advice into a therapeutic practice guided through the twists and turns of song."

A STOIC'S GUIDE TO A PHILOSOPHICAL PLAYLIST

SeThink is an influential contributor to West Indian music. Called the king of Shanto, a distinctively Guyanese calypso-style genre, his blogs often connect music to a diversity of disciplines. Curious about Stoicism, he read *A Guide to the Good Life: The Ancient Art of Stoic Joy* by William B. Irvine. Intrigued, that prompted him to further explore the writings of Seneca, Epictetus, and Marcus Aurelius. While not claiming to be a Stoic himself, he concluded the philosophy approximated his "approach" to life as well as any other. Relying on his musical proficiency while considering where music plays a part in Stoic life, he published on his blog in 2011 The Stoic's Songbook.[23]

While listening to *Dark Side of the Moon* takes listeners on a musical journey, SeThink brings another perspective, tapping into music that best embodies what the three great Stoic philosophers might say if they were on stage singing to adoring fans. While the entire catalog of popular music contains countless songs one could tie to this philosophy, the following are his picks. My hope is you find them therapeutic and learn more about Stoicism from an art form intent on soothing your soul while reinforcing why this school of thought matters.

1. "Murder in the City" by The Avett Brothers
2. "See These Bones" by Nada Surf
3. "Laughing With" by Regina Spektor
4. "Ill With Want" by The Avett Brothers
5. "The Right Place" by Monsters of Folk
6. "I Don't Want to Die (In the Hospital)" by Conor Oberst
7. "You Don't Miss Your Water" by Otis Redding
8. "World Keeps Turning" by Tom Waits

---

23 "The Stoic's Songbook." SeThink. March 6, 2011. https://sethink. wordpress.com/2011/03/06/the-stoics-songbook/.

CHAPTER 9

Maria Trusa:
To Forgive

Mwen pa di ankò. (Haitian Creole)
Je n'en dis pas plus. (French)
Eu digo não mais. (Portuguese)
Yo digo no más. (Spanish)
I say no more. (English)

"In the United States, every nine minutes, a child is sexually abused. Ninety-three percent of that abuse occurs at home."

Verb

1.   Stop feeling angry or resentful toward (someone) for an offense, flaw, or mistake.

Curious

Adjective

1.   Eager to know or learn something.

Founder of a movement and an organization called Yo Digo No Mas, Maria Trusa is a driven woman on a two-pronged mission:

1.   Deliver healthcare to the underserved, immigrant community.

2. Bring awareness to the silent pandemic of sexual abuse of children.

When asked why this cause, Maria fervently replied, "What makes sexual abuse even more dangerous is that no one wants to talk about it. The monster who is abusing the child is either their father, brother, uncle, or aunt. It is someone in the family."

> *"When those JFK airport doors opened, I thought to myself, Here I can be someone big. I will be someone important. Now is when my life begins. I was eager to start this new chapter. I also believed that God had much joy in store for me, because if I deserved penance for wrongdoing in this life, I had more than paid it after suffering through such a terrible incident. I wanted to continue believing that."[24]*

In her awe-inspiring book *I Say No More*, Maria described what it felt like for a fifteen-year-old girl raised in the Dominic Republic to arrive in the United States for the first time. Ready to transmute the tragedy of her past into the triumph that evolved into a wonderful life, Maria is the chief executive officer of Formé Medical Center and Urgent Care in White Plains, New York. She is also the architect of a crusade dedicated to ridding the world of child abuse.

Maria's dogged determination comes through in every fiber of her being. "My only purpose is to help women—and men too—face their personal demons and role in sexual abuse and take the first step. This is a tried-and-true formula

---

24 Trusa, Maria. "2." *I Say No More: My Story of Transformation from Abused Girl to Successful Woman*, 46–47. Middletown, DE: Independently published, 2020.

to overcome obstacles...honing my capacity to see the gift in every situation. I have learned to find the solution to any problem by visualizing the desired result and enjoying the process of getting there."

Understanding the origin of Maria's journey is best appreciated by the shocking and vicious event that happened to her in the Dominican Republic when she was nine years old. For context, Maria explained that it was commonplace in her native country to hear tales of local witches who made sacrifices of babies and children.

> The Santería religion fuses the Yoruba faith, practiced by African slaves, with Catholicism and the native customs of indigenous locals. But some deviant followers took it to another level by preying on the weak and abusing the people's trust. Rumors of kids being sacrificed in religious rituals traveled by word of mouth. She and her brothers were terrified of being kidnapped and taken away by a santero.[25]

As she narrates in Chapter 2 of her engrossing book, Maria describes what happened one fateful night when her father came home in his usual drunken stupor. This evening however was different because he was accompanied by a friend. Abruptly waking up Maria and her little brother Henry, they were suddenly staring at the other man referred to in their town as a witch. As he bent down to grab Henry, Maria struggled to take Henry back. Terrified as the events were unfolding, and screaming at the top of their lungs, the

---

25   Trusa, *I Say No More* (30).

witch had a sudden change of mind. Rather than Henry, Maria narrated in her book what happened next,

> *"The last thing I would have thought was that my father, the man who was supposed to take care of us, would place us in the hands of a criminal. His unbelievable act swiftly ended our childhoods in a macabre experience we all wish we could forget."*

"The unfolding scene was surreal. How was it possible my father was allowing this man to take me? Replacing my little brother was not the outcome I had in mind. Even though I didn't understand exactly what was meant by child sacrifice, I knew it was something terrible. My dad took me to a place where this man had built a small shed next to his house to carry out his rituals, a makeshift altar for evil. The brujo forced me to drink an entire bottle of whiskey and take some pills. I couldn't stop crying."

Threatening to kill her family if she said a word about this, the witch exerted an enormous power that left Maria feeling helpless. In agony and terrified at what else could happen,

"I could feel the alcohol burning me from within. I begged him for some water, but he refused. He had other ideas, cruel and disgusting plans to carry out without the least bit of remorse. I knew his wife and kids were in the house. I cried as loudly as I could, hoping someone would hear me and come to my rescue. But no one stirred, no one cared to help."

"The true horror began once we entered the motel room, far worse than anything I had experienced until then. He had me cornered and made me stop crying to avoid causing a bigger scene. I understood there was no point in continuing since nothing could stop him now."

> *"As soon as the door closed, he began touching me. The pain I felt grew bigger and deeper. It was a knife piercing my soul, plunging into me a thousand times over. It was not only the pain of knowing that this monster was hurting me physically, but knowing he was killing my innocence, stealing my childhood, and contaminating each phase of my life into adulthood. That cruel beast took for himself the right to my child's body, my life, and my future."*

Maria further described the continued torture and anguish as blood seemed to be rushing from every direction. As she was burning inside and feeling torn to pieces, the witch dropped her back at home the next morning as if nothing happened.

> *"It is incredible to think how much suffering and destruction a brutal, inhumane, and selfish act such as rape could provoke. I have learned of abuse victims who fell into drug use and never recovered. Others opted to end their lives because they simply could not move forward afterwards. How has such a perverse act become so commonplace?"*

Maria and her brothers recalled "how long and hard my mom fought to put the man who raped me in jail and throw away the key. Unfortunately, she never succeeded. I am deeply saddened to think how many times he got away with such atrocities; how many other lives he ruined. Although today, thanks be to God, I can proudly say that my life has not been destroyed."

> *"I felt abandoned as a child then suffered a gruesome violation. But arriving in this country created new hope and the chance to turn my dreams into reality. I took control of rewriting my destiny."*

From that fateful night, Maria documented in her book the insights she carries with her each day:

- The past can keep our heads underwater as we drag others along for the ride.

- We can spend so much time playing the victim, it becomes the only thing we know.

- To properly understand our lives, we must recognize what our parents and grandparents endured as reasons why our childhoods played out as they did.

- A parent's bad decisions and poor choices set off a chain reaction.

- The disease of addiction does not enter any home alone.

- Alcohol is a powerful drug. Combined with ignorance, the consequences of abuse are limitless.

"Surviving that night in flesh and spirit is what gave me the compassion and desire to empower women and create a movement to battle this can-

*cer. I am still here, motivated to act against sexual
abuse in all its forms."*

Several years after that horrendous night, living in the
New York City area, Maria experienced marriage, career
growth, and motherhood. From the moment she became a
mom, she made the decision to overcome the toxic residue
of her childhood experience and to...

- Change her role from victim to protagonist.
- Become the heroine of her own story.
- Take control of her life and rewrite the painful
  narrative as one of realization and triumph.

Telling Maria's story "was not easy." It took forty-seven
years to document it. Loved ones encouraged her that doing
so, "no matter how difficult, could become the catalyst that
would inspire others—especially women—to tell their stories too." Their voices could rise together to:

- Condemn abuse in its many forms.
- Help transcend their wounds.
- Live a full life as they are meant to.

When she reflects years later the event that destroyed her
innocence, it became a driving force in her ambition to protect all children from the horrors of sexual abuse.

When Maria considered the insufferable event that
shaped her adult thinking, "I was disgusted being a Dominican. It is because of that life chapter that I did not want to
go back. I missed my country. But I did not want to return to

that fear. I was there for six more years after that happened. I lived with the horror of seeing that man. He went to jail for three months and got out."

Reflecting on the transition into her American life, her teenage journey in America helped her to look at life differently. She decided to take control of her decisions and learn to say NO. "

MARIA'S TURNING POINT

Much of the pain Maria recounts was driven by the relationship she had with her father. "Since the moment he ripped me into the hands of that monster, nighttime became synonymous with danger, pain, and terror." Through the years, Maria was still "badly broken." When she recounts the circumstances of that gruesome night...

> "The worst part of this event was my father's indifference and cruelty."

"After my son was born, my father was dying. Given a brain tumor, he could not speak. My uncle called me to say my dad was on his death bed. He wants to ask for your forgiveness. When I gave it, my uncle said he cried, then took his last breath. He went with my forgiveness."

This became Maria's next big accelerator and showed her two things:

I. Her heart opened. She wanted to ask him, "How could you do that?" When he asked for forgiveness, she was the last person on his mind before he died.

He gave her an insight into his pain, and it did not matter anymore. He did not have to explain it.

2. The other piece...how "crazy" she was to let herself hate all those years. She "hated him with a vengeance; could not even look at his picture. He was the devil, and with me every day!

"I worked to eliminate any trace of hate left in my heart, knowing such negative feelings and emotions jeopardize personal growth. Once we forgive, we fill ourselves with an inner peace no one can take from us. Forgiveness is an exercise in self-reflection and provides instant feedback. It is the gift that keeps on giving. Such a kind and loving act can only generate inner peace for both the forgiver and forgiven."[26]

---

26   Trusa, Maria. "2." *I Say No More.*

After her father passed, Maria realized she had been carrying that animosity into the disconnect with her son. Coming from social norms that lead her to be submissive... cook, clean, serve the king, she began to question, "Why do I have to attend to this man when I, too, am working?" The more she questioned, the more curious she became about her future.

Maria's curiosity started to grow, now questioning her marriage. "I am putting up with someone who abuses me mentally, physically, and cheats on me all the time." When she had her second child, she discovered he was cheating on her with a friend. That was it—another turning point, another accelerator.

> *"I became more emotionally intelligent by developing a ferocious curiosity."*

From then on, Maria initiated a torrent of personal and professional development. From high school completion to medical assistance training, she "was releasing those negative emotions that block people from having focus and clarity. You begin to see other possibilities."

Maria's training led her to Scarsdale Medical Group, where for twenty-six years she was preparing for her next milestone, CEO. Recounting the gratitude she felt to capitalize on opportunities that presented themselves, the "curiosity opens your eyes more. I came from nothing. However, I started bringing that curiosity to work. Can I learn this? Can I learn that? I am now in a place where people recognize my hard work. Little by little, I wanted to give more." From medical assistant, to manager, to executive director overseeing a $5 million company, Maria was on the mend and career climbing like never before.

"I redirected and focused on self-respect and self-worth."

On further examination, Maria came to a life-altering conclusion that forgiving her father was the catalyst that unleashed her massive burst of creativity. Although she could not have predicted it, this inspired her and sustained the drive to contribute to every life she touched. "Once I stopped judging myself, it increased my capacity to be more curious. For instance, I used to think the doctors I worked with were gods. They came from schools like Columbia, spoke well, and had so much money. By being more curious, I learned about their family situations and their suffering. From that curiosity they became human. I suddenly was saying to myself we're not that different." She started to relate to everyone around in ways she had hardly imagined.

"Applying these lessons helped me defend myself and confront others when I needed to without feeling inferior. I always held my head high. And why shouldn't I?"

It significantly increased her empathy, a critical part of her Emotional Intelligence development.

Maria subsequently started to rely on the sum of those horrific experiences to feel what others feel. She understood the sources of others' pain and could empathize in ways she could not have predicted. Attuned to body language and the silent cues offered, she found it easier to feel their energy and connect in new and distinct ways. She felt the power of becoming more emotional intelligent and converted that energy into a movement that has shaped her extraordinary life. Recognizing she could not build this movement alone, she learned to take care of herself so that she was able to give so much more to others.

> *"Each person I met helped shape me into the person I see before me in the mirror."*

As Maria gained clarity on the impact that forgiveness had on her, she "better understood its value and immense healing power." She subsequently wrote in her book additional lessons for parents and children alike:

- A genuine connection between a parent and child is based on respect.
- Most believe a parent's status as an adult implies the need to be obeyed.
- Title alone does not command respect. It needs to be earned.
- Respect your child's way of thinking, ideas, and beliefs, and especially their decisions, which are as legitimate and valid as yours.

Self-Awareness	Self-Management	Social Awareness	Relationship Management
Assessment	Self-Control	Empathy	Conflict Management
Confidence	Transparency	Service to Others	Collaboration
	Adaptability		Influence

Maria's transformation ultimately led her to pursue a calling that tugged at her for some time—to fill the need for proper healthcare for her Latino community. But even more potent, she learned to speak her goals into existence. To do that, "The most important element to gain support for your idea is conviction. With that, you can achieve anything."

CALL TO ACTION

When Maria considered the impact of forgiving her father, she realized he was a victim of those who came before him. Still, she articulates in her book, lessons applicable to anyone on either side of forgiveness:

1. **The Challenge and Impact of Forgiveness**

    - Many stuck with negative feelings physically manifest their emotions by getting sick.
    - Identify repressed emotions and bring them to light.
    - Recognize and accept your feelings as real.
    - It may take a while, but the day of reckoning will come.
    - Compassion and empathy are superpowers—put yourself in their shoes.
    - Forgiveness has no expiration date.
    - Let go!

The series of events in Maria's life aligns perfectly with how the Stoics think about the concept of forgiveness. Marcus

Aurelius reminded himself that people who do us wrong do so because they have been deprived of truth and philosophy (like her father). He wrote, "The best way to avenge yourself is to not be like that." According to Epictetus, "Forgive others for their misdeeds over and over again." Adding to Maria's growth in Self-Awareness, he also said, "Forgive ourselves repeatedly. Then try to do better next time."

2. Face Your Demons; Do Not Run From Them

Maria came to learn the hard way that any major issue, if left unresolved, will eventually rear its ugly head. Secrets, denial, and deflection will not solve any problem. Sweeping them under the rug may feel good for a time, but eventually it will catch up to everyone involved. Her message then is clear. Speak up in the spirt of candor and good will so you can help prevent other family members from falling prey to a similar fate.

It takes a lot of discipline to achieve this Stoic control, but it provides an effective way to cope with life's events, both joyous and infuriating. When life gets hard, we often look for ways to escape and hide from them. Seneca says, "You must shed the load that is on your mind: until you do that, no place will be pleasing to you." In the Self-Management dimension of EQ, Maria leads by example that honesty is the best policy. She is transparent in every aspect of her life, courageously confronting the uncomfortable and recognizing the importance of addressing interpersonal conflicts before they escalate into something more dire.

3. Every Act, Good or Bad, Becomes Our Best Teachers

"The highs and lows of life, those swift changes that bring loss and new beginning, are the best teachers of willpower, inner strength, flexibility, and bravery." Summarizing her mindset shift from victim to protagonist, Maria offers:

- No one makes or breaks us.

- We are responsible for how we react to what happens.

- The only author of your story is you.

Maria came to understand over the years how every lesson is a gift. As Marcus Aurelius stated, "All you need are certainty of judgment in the present moment, action for the common good, and an attitude of gratitude for anything that comes your way." She continually expresses thankfulness and appreciation for the remarkable people in her life. Epictetus says, "The key is to keep company only with people who uplift you, whose presence calls forth your best."

Maria's Top Ten Life Guidelines

1. No one can ruin my life.

2. If I can believe it, I can achieve it.

3. Demonstrate conviction in all things.

4. Let go of the illusion of control.

5. Respond with love and kindness to anyone who comes your way.

6. You catch more flies with honey than vinegar.

7. Forget wanting to be right all the time.

8. Say the Magic word, *Please.*

9. Wish love and light on others.

10. Strive to maintain inner peace.

> *"Learning to control ourselves and being present in the moment is the only path to personal fulfillment and to treating others especially our loves ones, with kindness and respect."*

Additional Insights to Increase Self- and Social-Awareness

- Ego will take control of your life if you are not aware of it.

- If a situation is not dire, allow them the freedom to make their own mistakes and the time to find themselves.

- If you maintain a calm demeanor and avoid backlash, opting instead for empathy and patience, your relationships will get back on track.

- Personal growth starts with a desire to look within, a tickling curiosity that becomes an overpowering need to know why we feel one way or another. From there everything falls into place.

- What I learned in my journey of self-discovery, is to put all my energy into situations I can control.

- When I have no control, accept it, and let it go.

To accelerate her Emotional Intelligence growth, she listened to the Stoics, who advised their followers to put themselves in the other person's shoes—understand their perspective before passing judgment. As Marcus Aurelius said, "When you face someone's insults, hatred, whatever, look at his soul. Get inside him. Look at what sort of person he is. You'll find you don't need to strain to impress him."

Parental Emotional Intelligence Lessons

- Reflect on our behaviors and reactions because others—especially children—are not responsible for our history.
- It is not their burden to carry.
- We always have a choice as parents to improve and do better for our children.
- If we come from a sincere place with the purpose of wanting our children to carry our legacy, we can achieve anything with them.
- Learn to listen to your children without judgment.
- Make sure they always feel protected.
- Give them time. Step back and respect their wishes.
- Maintain proper expectations.

"I have gained the wisdom to understand it is never too late to heal and rebuild a connection with your children. God gave me a gift of tuning into people, especially my children."

The sum of Maria's life events resulted in some extraordinary outcomes. She...

- Developed more profound and interesting relationships.
- Discovered loyal friends.
- Enjoyed more dedicated co-workers.
- Gained greater recognition in her industry.
- Increased her finances considerably.

While noting her top two accelerators were the experience with her son and finding herself on the brink of death, "My entire world grew with me, proving repeatedly that prioritizing our inner selves is the best investment we can make. Yet, perhaps I had not set the bar high enough. God called attention to autopilot mode without reaching my full potential, making me realize our most prized possession is life itself."

> *"Our goal is to discover the niche created especially for us, to sharpen our skills and abilities. When God places a dream and a mission in your heart, He will never leave you alone in the process of fulfilling it."*

The goal of Stoicism is to live a happy and smoothly flowing life. To achieve this, we strive to live up to our natural inborn potential, always reaching higher and expressing what we are capable of every moment. A key tenet of this philosophy is living with virtue, or "excellence." As Seneca

THE MOMENT THAT DEFINES YOUR LIFE

the Younger said, "A good character is the only guarantee of everlasting, carefree happiness."

While running a multimillion-dollar enterprise is not always carefree, Maria has achieved a level of equanimity and inner peace. Purpose-driven, passionate, and committed to fulfilling a mission, her message to the world is loud and clear. "I SAY NO MORE. Together we can eradicate the scourge of rape, abuse, and rampant misogyny that destroys lives. Don't be another statistic. Break your silence, raise your voice. Become the exception to the rule and transform your pain into personal success. Rewrite your life."

> *"I can proudly say that my life will continue to be limitless. This is the legacy I want to leave my family."*

On May 3, 2019, Maria returned to the motel where the brutal assault occurred. "In all those years, I have never been able to even look at the motel from a distance. This time, I had the courage to go in. I feel free today. Today, my favorite word is unstoppable. The abominable act that could have destroyed me provided more strength than I knew possible. We have a responsibility to share the best of ourselves with others, what has made our lives better and helped us rise from the ashes of adversity."

For your consideration: Shop Films creates compelling programming demonstrating the magic of the human spirit in overcoming life's trials and realizing accomplishment. The goal is to bring viewers "from tears to cheers with an appreciation of entrepreneurial behavior." Their purpose is to provide programming that "relays the transformative power of entrepreneurship." While their featured subjects encountered adversity most of us only hear about, Maria shares her story of child abuse, teen pregnancy, language barriers, poverty, near-death illness, and unfaithful spouses and says, "My story is everyone's story." To learn more and watch this powerful and compelling documentary, click *Trauma to Triumph Featuring Maria Trusa*. As noted in the film,

> *"Maria is a woman who reclaimed and restored her life; converting it into a beaming beacon of light for others."*[27]

---

27   "About." Trauma to Triumph. https://traumatotriumphfilms.com/about/.

CHAPTER 10

Rajesh Setty:
To Outsee

Transitive Verb

1. To surpass in power of vision or insight.

2. To see beyond.

When scaling a mountain, it is easy to be blindsided by fear. To a first-timer, looking up is terrifying. The anxiety leads many climbers to stop dead in their tracks. Thoughts of "I don't know why I signed on" invade the senses as a litany of doubts floods their mind. The only way forward is reverse. Turning around and heading home feels awfully good. Sensing they had enough, other climbers sadly view that action as an admission of defeat. Or, if they did not reach the summit, the mission was a failure. Whether success or failure, Stoics treat them as one and the same. Success is not defined by the outcome but by the process. That way, it is always in their control, with no need to attach their self-worth to the result.

Whether climbing or living at sea level, there is one person in my life who finds himself on a proverbial mountain. He pays no mind to success or failure. Summit or not, he may turn around. It doesn't matter. Whichever way he goes is forward. It's not because he refuses to fail—on the contrary. He will not stop. He leads by example and lives with a set of guiding principles I admire and emulate. What makes him extraordinary has nothing to do with mountaineering. However, I can't help but see the parallels in how he reacts to unexpected events that are similar in mindset to how I feel on my most treacherous mountains. He has the capacity to see beyond limitations and has chosen a distinct approach to live a generous and fulfilling life no matter the circumstances.

His name is Rajesh Setty. His story is powerful, compelling, and redefines what it means to be resilient. His intellect, work ethic, and professional standards are exceeded only by his overwhelming generosity to people in his orbit. To categorize Rajesh does not do him justice. But I'll try. He is a serial entrepreneur, has written eighteen books, and co-founded Audvisor, a mobile audio streaming app from world-class experts. He is a philosopher and the most emotionally intelligent man I know. While Rajesh dedicates his life to the service of others, knowing how he reacts to any given situation underscores why he is, in my humble opinion, the modern-day Marcus Aurelius.

Before I examine what makes Rajesh incomparable, he is on a proverbial mountain climb that is more challenging than Mount Everest and K2 combined. His life parallels mountaineering in three ways:

1. When caught in those moments of "go ahead or turn around," no matter what you decide, the most important step is the next one. The only certainty

in the life of a mountaineer is having the option to climb one more rung in either direction. You may not know where that step will touch the ground. But recognize one consideration: Despite the most trying conditions, you will find the resolve to take it. Never mind poor conditions, fatigue, or injury; the will to prevail inspires you to climb on. That mindset motivates you to step up in those moments when all you want is to lie down.

2. Mountaineering tests your limits. With many factors beyond your control, you decide with each step whether climbing is the smartest or dumbest decision ever made. When you think the ascent gets easier, it turns on you in an instant and feels like the world's most formidable task. Through it all, you find the strength that seemed inconceivable moments earlier. Despite the ice ax, rope, and crampons, you are sustained by the mind's capacity to find the strength to push through limits you did not know you had. Even when you think you have reached them, there is more to give.

3. As you exceed expectations, reveling in those bursts of self-confidence, you believe with each step you will prevail. However, negative thoughts can surface out of nowhere, forcing you to use the power of your mind to keep climbing. Throughout the journey it is natural to see beyond and place yourself at the top even when things are not going well. As Marcus Aurelius said, "Your ability to control your

thoughts—treat it with respect. It's all that protects your mind from false perceptions—false to your nature, and that of all rational beings. It's what makes thoughtfulness possible, and affection for other people, and submission to the divine."

There is no shortcut in mountaineering. There is no climb, career, or calling that can be accomplished solo. Hence, the quality of your guides, mates, and friends is a major factor in how you perceive the experience—good, bad, or indifferent. There is no greater honor than to climb with like-minded people who are selfless and unyielding in their quest to serve a mission. This metaphor sums up what it is like to be in the presence of Rajesh.

In addition to his magnificent philosophy and life lessons, he is a powerful, proverbial mountain guide. Features of his life approach are:

- His passion is "to bring good and game-changing ideas to life with love."
- His heart "sings when an idea comes to life that makes the world a better place."
- He has failed "a *lot*" and learned from each failure. Because of them, he succeeded many times in all kinds of business endeavors.

To sum up his LinkedIn bio, he is a "work in progress." He guarantees his work but leaves "the progress to God."

Rajesh's moment is made more powerful when you step back and analyze the timeline and the "Energizer bunny" vigor he exuded from a young age. To grasp the potency of Rajesh's moment, it is best to understand the exceptional drive and performance he exhibited from the conception of his first passion—reading books. By nine years old he read almost seven hundred. The way he describes it sounds like an addiction. He learned in his youth if he had time to read, he would have to "learn how to learn fast." He is only desire was for more time to read and learn outside his formal studies.

His passionate drive to consume novels rapidly evolved into a pursuit of writing and publishing his own material. By age ten, he took eight months to write his first novel. He followed that up with an impressive effort to contact publishing houses. Within a few years, after 160 rejections, he published his first book—a murder mystery. While this achievement is astonishing, it sets the stage for a man who, from an astoundingly young age, was "pedal to the metal" driven to learn, create, and execute his ideas. Moving forward quickly was the name of his game. He states, "I did not have time to reflect because I was always busy. Anything that caught my fancy, I would go deep in it." By seventeen he had published six books.

An engineer by trade, he made a series of career moves in Asia. Thinking globally, he visited northern California and fell in love with the Silicon Valley culture. Rajesh flexed his entrepreneurial wings in 2000 and founded a startup. He became a leadership figure, not because he was naturally driven to seek it, but because no one else was willing to take the risk and commit to learning while on their business journey. Rajesh relentlessly pushed forward with his startup, failed fast, and learned even quicker what not to do.

By 2014 at the age of forty-four, he noticed what felt like a relatively innocent symptom—a tingling sensation whenever he yawned. This became the harbinger of what would become an unexpected medical diagnosis. After six months of useless creams prescribed to relieve it, a neurologist referred him to Stanford University Hospital for tests. After a grueling six-hour examination the doctor said, "You have Parkinson's Disease. Any questions?"

Rajesh was speechless in the moment that defined the rest of his life. A man that lived pedal to the metal in pursuit of his passions, constantly climbing proverbial mountains at the speed of light, was forced to slow down.

The diagnosis did not settle in immediately. He knew it was bad, but because of his positive attitude, he was unsure to what degree. He took time to reflect and, like a mountaineer, considered his next step. He continually called on his mantra,

"I'm here. Where next?"

He allowed time to accept the diagnosis, knowing he could not fight the truth. No matter how hard he struggled with the diagnosis, it did not change his reality. "I'm here"—acceptance of the situation. "Where next?"—engaging in a mentality of wonder with each next step.

For context, Parkinson's is a progressive, neurodegenerative disorder. It is a lifelong condition that affects the brain whose symptoms worsen over time. Parkinson's occurs when brain cells that produce dopamine stop working or die. Dopamine is a chemical that sends messages between nerve and muscle cells to help the body function. Referred to as a neurotransmitter, it plays many roles in the body and affects physical and mental functions. The cardinal symptoms of Parkinson's are tremors, slowness of movement, and difficulty balancing. Because these indicators are related to movement, they are called "motor symptoms." Hence, Parkinson's is classified as a "movement disorder." Symptoms are unique to an individual. Although there is no cure, treatments are offered to manage the symptoms and improve the quality of life.

In good times and in bad, humans hate change and resist it most of the time. But Rajesh did not have a choice. He could not repel the powerful force in motion. This did not stop him. It slowed him down physically but empowered him mentally. He adjusted his perspective on life to find joy and actively engage in chosen activities. He did not slip into the "woe is me" attitude for one moment. He took time to acknowledge the diagnosis, then worked on moving ahead. "I'm here; where next?"

Rajesh's ability to reframe his perspective was the catalyst for change. As I considered others whose lives were in extremis, Rajesh's outlook reminded me of what I took away from Viktor Frankl's book, *Man's Search for Meaning*, "If you find a why, then you can bear any how." Frankl and Rajesh agree if you know your purpose, you can overcome any challenge that life hands you.

This was the first time in Rajesh's life that he had no choice but to slow down and smell the roses. He was living through a profound change and overall viewpoint on well-being. He was involved in multiple companies, had written several books, and taught in many places. Suddenly, it all came to a screeching halt. He realized that moving slower allowed him to observe the world around him with a higher fidelity. He could now take the time to think, reflect, and see more clearly.

For a glimpse of Rajesh's philosophy, I turn to one of his books called *Outsee: Spot game-changing opportunities early and often*. From the start, he provokes the reader to consider an important question:

"Are you struggling to make a big impact?"

No matter what you do, you can't seem to get beyond that plateau. Many of you have given up on the fact you cannot make it big. If you are one of them, consider two things:

1. You are not alone.
2. It's not your fault.

Society's focus seems to be on taking good actions. If people do what smart, successful people have done, prosperity follows. Nothing is further than the truth. Some people go one step beyond. They believe what precedes action is thinking. If they can mimic those high achievers, similar gains await. Most people stop there.

But...there is magic to take one more step. Seeing precedes thinking. What you see sets the boundaries for your thoughts, not the other way around. With visual clarity, you realize more possibilities.

BEFORE YOU CAN OUTTHINK AND OUTPERFORM, YOU MUST OUTSEE

Outsee sets the possibilities and provides a competitive edge. You see the power of outsee in your life all the time. When you share a problem with someone successful, within moments they help you see things you do not. To you this may be an "aha moment." To them, it's another day at the office.

He subsequently provides a framework on how to outsee. Comprising his tool kit are proverbial...

- Kaleidoscope: Diversified external input on your problem, situation, or the possibilities you are examining.

- Telescope: Looking at the big picture, borrowing lessons from elsewhere, and recrafting it to your situation.

- Microscope: The science of dissection. Look at what happens before, during, and after a value exchange point.

- Gyroscope: Describes what is happening despite your blind spots.

- Periscope: Looking at trends coming down the pike, and taking advantage of those strengths before others.

- Thermostat: How to create or reconfigure what you already have so new possibilities emerge.

Rajesh asserts, "When you learn to outsee, you welcome a new world of possibilities."

By helping others to see beyond, Rajesh is the gold standard for Self-Awareness. He exudes self-confidence regardless of any situation. Through the diagnosis, he fine-tuned his emotional state. He became keenly aware of the emotional complexities stirring inside and distilled them into a sense of understanding that is astonishing. In the words of Viktor Frankl, "Everything can be taken from a man but one thing: the last of the human freedoms—to choose one's attitude in any given set of circumstances, to choose one's own way."

Self-Awareness	Self-Management	Social Awareness	Relationship Management
Assessment	Self-Control	Empathy	Conflict Management
Confidence	Transparency	Service to Others	Collaboration
	Adaptability		Influence

For Self-Management, Rajesh may as well teach a master class. He learned to keep disruptive emotions in check and handle the challenges with power and grace. In the words of Epictetus, "Happiness and freedom begin with a clear understanding of one principle: Some things are within your control. And some things are not." He followed that by saying, "People are not upset by things, but by the judgments they have about things." The Stoics then strike a chord on two aspects that relate to Rajesh's arc:

- You create your own reality.
- The concept of indifference.

Rajesh saw his condition as an opportunity to reframe the condition—trying to look at it from a different perspective to change subsequent feelings and behaviors. Seeing beyond... indifferent to Parkinson's. Rather than regarding good health as the benchmark for all things happy, the Stoics tell a different story. Their philosophical premise is that the supreme good in life is a virtue, of which Rajesh possesses an abundance. Illness is no longer seen as the devil that weighed him down, to feel less than others. His attitude is self-empowered, lacking any notion of a victim mentality.

Rajesh recognizes that life can be as free or as tethered as you perceive it. When you consider a situation, you see the past. Because it happened, each event is interpreted for better or worse. The memories are locked indelibly in your mind; the future is not. Anything forthcoming is indeterminate, which to some is frightening. To Rajesh, however, he sees beyond and teaches others to do the same. Never a burden; seeing beyond is an opportunity to discover a world of endless possibilities.

Consequently, he stresses there are two ways to cope with the uncertainty of a diagnosis: acceptance or resistance. Acceptance allows events to unfold around you and to react to them spontaneously, without suppression. With resistance you try hard to change events and react with familiar, safe responses. Acceptance is healthy as it permits you to clear the stress as it occurs. Resistance is not, as anxiety develops frustration, false expectations, and unfulfilled desires.

I sense if Rajesh authors another book, his insights into others working through a chronic condition would offer a fresh perspective and renewed sense of self-esteem, resilience, and pride. Consequently, I see a vision beyond Sunnyvale in 2023.

In the future, on stage in front of thousands, Rajesh chairs a panel of experts, including Epictetus, Seneca, and Marcus Aurelius. They have come together to share insights on what it is like to approach illness from the Stoic's point of view. In the spirit of Rajesh's book *Outsee*, Epictetus looks at the enormous crowd and communicates with clarity and encouragement, "Sickness is a problem for the body, not the mind—unless the mind decides that it is a problem. Lameness, too, is the body's problem, not the mind's. Say this to yourself whatever the circumstance and you will find without fail that the problem pertains to something else, not to you."

Seneca picks up on his colleague's statement and exclaims, "Illness has actually given many people a new lease on life; the experience of being near to death has been their preservation. You will die not because you are sick but because you are alive. That end still awaits you when you have been cured."

Marcus, patiently awaiting his turn, takes a deep breath, regards the crowd, and with great power and purpose says, "It's fortunate that this has happened, and I've remained unharmed by it—not shattered by the present or frightened of the future. It could have happened to anyone. But not everyone could have remained unharmed by it."

Rajesh then thanks his guests for spending time with all of them. In a flash of gratitude and goodwill, he looks at his mates, stares into the crowd, and says with great enthusiasm and aplomb the advice his friend Marcus offered when he heard Rajesh was diagnosed with Parkinson's Disease.

"While it's true that someone can impede our actions, they can't impede our intentions and our attitudes, which have the power of being conditional and adaptable. For the mind adapts and converts any obstacle to its action into a means of achieving it. That which is an impediment to action is turned to advance action. The obstacle on the path becomes the way."

Rajesh then looks up to God and quietly says, "Thank *you* for helping me find the path that became my way."

CALL TO ACTION

To Outsee

Consider how the world has changed in one generation:

- A Google search takes milliseconds. In my college days, the same task took hours, if not days.

- Buy a book with one click. It saves a drive to Barnes & Noble, where I was frequently told, "We are out of stock."

- I can record a high-quality video on a Mac computer and edit it in minutes. Before that Apple invention, I had to hire someone, rent studio time, and wait for the first cut. No more.

Such are the joys of these astonishing inventions. How did we get here?

Take a moment to ponder who created the modern world. A few names surface most of the time: Larry Page, Jeff Bezos, and Steve Jobs. When you look them up online, note the adjectives people use to describe them and the similarities are striking. "Visionary," "bold," and "risk-taker" appear often, in addition to "intelligence," "strong organizational skills," and "exquisite execution." Each of their companies emerged from a similar place: A blank sheet of paper with an idea and a desire to, as Steve Jobs said, "Put a dent in the universe."

They were independent thinkers and resisted the herd mentality. We learned from the Stoics the power of assigning things their proper value and not being held captive by what others think. They knew the importance of identifying what was within their control, what was beyond, and what fell in between. And they maintained an unwavering sense of focus on the things within their realm of control.

According to the *Daily Stoic*, a Stoic "has to be willing to do that...to think for themself. A Stoic doesn't care what the mob thinks—they don't need to 'consort with the crowd' as Seneca put it. Yes, it's wonderful that we have access to all kinds of knowledge and tools that the Stoics didn't have. But how we use these assets is essential. Are we just going to agree with everyone because we don't want trouble? Are we going to seek out only what we like and what confirms our worldview?" Stoics consequently developed their own worldview and executed career and life plans accordingly.

When you study the great entrepreneurs that came one hundred years earlier, Ford, Carnegie, and Rockefeller come to mind. It is not a big leap to suggest they, too, were visionary, bold, and risk-takers. As I watched the TV series *The Men Who Built America* on the History Channel, these men and their organizations transformed every industry they touched. History keeps repeating itself.

One other characteristic applies to both the nineteenth and twentieth-century visionaries that doesn't always appear in the countless books and articles written about them. They were able to outsee, to surpass in power of vision or insight so many others with similar ideas. Perhaps their competitors we had never heard of were trapped by their nature, dogma, or ideology. Maybe they thought conventionally. Or, felt they had all the answers. Some assert, however, they had a narrower field of vision, thwarting their range and limiting their opportunities. They did not outsee!

Credit is often given to one man who built the bridge between companies that emerged in the Industrial Revolution and those created one hundred years later. His name is Peter Drucker. He, too, had an immense capacity to outsee and failed not on his answers but on the ignorance of his questions. According to the Claremont Graduate University Drucker School of Management, he "crossed many boundaries as a writer, teacher, management consultant, and business visionary. He has been called 'the inventor of modern management' for good reason. He believed in business as a human-driven enterprise that could be profitable *and* socially responsible.... From his early beginnings as a financial reporter in Frankfurt, Germany to his pioneering study of General Motors and the book that made his name—*The Concept of the Corporation*—Dr. Drucker has changed how we see business."[28]

Drucker pioneered the idea of privatization and the corporation as a social institution. He coined the terms "knowledge worker" and "management by objective." His seminal study of General Motors published in 1946 introduced the concept of decentralization as an organizational principle, in contrast to the practice of command and control in business. According to the *McKinsey Quarterly* in 1997, "In the world of management gurus, there is no debate. Peter Drucker is the one guru to whom other gurus kowtow."

What did we learn most from Peter Drucker? In 1976 at a lecture at Claremont College, William A. Cohen, a longtime protégé of his, recounts in his book *A Class with Drucker: The Lost Lessons of the World's Greatest Management Teacher*: "Drucker began to reminisce about his work with various corporations both here and in Japan. He told us that it was often simple things an outsider could do to have a major impact on the company he assisted. This was because inside people were generally too close to the issues, and also because they assumed things from their past experience they incorrectly thought were identical in the present situation. An outsider would wonder and question these things that a practicing manager in the organization frequently missed."[29]

28 "Peter F. Drucker Claremont Graduate University." Claremont Graduate University, July 19, 2018. https://www.cgu.edu/school/drucker-school-of-management/peter-f-drucker/.
29 "Peter Drucker on the Value of Ignorance." AMA. Accessed July 3, 2023. https://www.amanet.org/articles/peter-drucker-on-the-value-of-ignorance/.

When asked about the secret of success, Drucker responded, "There is no secret. You just need to ask the right questions. Unexpectedly, one of my students raised his arm and exploded with three questions in rapid succession. 'How do you know the right questions to ask? Aren't your questions based on the knowledge in the industries in which you consult? How did you have the knowledge and expertise to do this when you were first starting out with no experience?"

Drucker's response: "I never ask questions or approach these assignments based on my knowledge and experience in these industries....It is exactly the opposite. I do not use my knowledge and experience at all. I bring my ignorance to the situation. Ignorance is the most important component for helping others to solve a problem in any industry."

Drucker emphasized he had access to the same information as everyone else. And never claimed to know more than the people who hired him. His capacity to outsee and provoke extraordinary change in corporate behavior was counter-intuitive to what most people were typically taught. In Drucker's mind, too much knowledge clouded their field of vision inhibiting the capacity to outsee.

> *"Ignorance is not such a bad thing if one knows how to use it... You must approach problems with your ignorance; not what you think you know from past experience, because frequently, what you think you know is wrong."*

Questioning was a crucial part of Drucker's repertoire. He is famous for what he articulates in his bestselling book *Peter Drucker's Five Most Important Questions: Enduring Wisdom for Today's Leaders.* Questioning was a core principle of his approach as a consultant. Author, speaker, and blogger Bruce Rosenstein builds on the foundation of Drucker's questioning techniques in his insightful book *Living in More than One World: How Peter Drucker's Wisdom Can Inspire and Transform Your Life.* He provokes readers to think differently about their lives and articulates a series of questions that relate to Rajesh's framework on how to outsee.

TO OUTSEE: NOT ANSWERS, BUT QUESTIONS

The capacity to outsee means asking better questions. Or, asking what no one thought of or was too afraid to offer. Before you consider how to outsee others and capitalize on your ideas, ask yourself some questions from Rosenstein's book to challenge and uproot your conventional thinking.

> From Chapter 1: **Designing Your Total Life:** *Is there a mentor or a friend I could contact to give me ideas on how to add more multidimensionality to my life?*

> From Chapter 2: **Developing Your Core Competencies:** *What is a particular lesson learned from my early work experience that is so powerful I will never forget it?*

> From Chapter 3: **Creating Your Future:** *How would my choice of a second career differ from my first? What specifically do I admire about people*

who have reinvented their lives? What can I learn from their experience that would give me ideas for my possible reinvention?

When I consider some of the lessons I learned from Drucker, Rosenstein, and Rajesh, the capacity to outsee starts with what not to do:

- Follow in someone else's footsteps.
- Apply another's recipe for success.
- Focus on what your competition is doing.

Many blockbuster entrepreneurs achieved astonishing success by developing something no one else did before them. They outsaw others and executed with extraordinary speed and conviction to turn their dreams into reality.

To reinforce these behaviors, I often turn to the bards whose ways with words inspire, ignite change, and remind us that to outsee, questions, not answers, rule the day. As Rudyard Kipling prompts us in his poetry:

"I keep six honest serving men

They taught me all I knew;

Their names are What and Why and When

And How and Where and Who."

EPILOGUE

Chuck Garcia:
To Lose (Yourself)

1. Be deprived of or cease to have or retain (something).

2. Become unable to find (something or someone).

What do music, mountains, and moments have in common? At first glance, not a lot. But on further examination...

Scan the QR code to pull up the lyrics to "Lose Yourself" by Eminem.

Mount Elbrus is the highest and most prominent peak in Russia. Located in the western part of the Caucasus Mountains on the Georgian border, the dormant volcano stands 18,510 feet above sea level. Jagged peaks with glaciers flow gracefully into fertile valleys. The summit offers breathtaking views feeling like the world is at your doorstep. Two events are credited with putting Elbrus on the mountaineering map. In 1829, Killar Khashirov reached the eastern summit. The higher western side was subsequently summitted by a British expedition in 1874.

MOUNT ELBRUS
RUSSIA, CAUCASUS MOUNTAINS

On the morning of August 14, 2014, I reached the western summit. Guided by a company called Mountain Madness based in Seattle, Washington, our team had nine climbers from the US, Australia, and South Africa. We were led by three extraordinary guides and reached the peak in eleven days. The experience landed somewhere on a continuum between exhilaration and exhaustion. Standing at the top, I barely had the energy to snap a photo of my Australian mate Danny Klima. Painfully aware of my desire to descend, he grinned from ear to ear and encouraged me to "take it in. Enjoy the view." With some deep breaths the pain subsided long enough to enjoy the vista. Sharing that moment with us were teams from Norway and Japan. With hugs, high fives, and summit talk in several languages, we enjoyed the panorama and prepared to head back to the village where the expedition began.

When I started climbing mountains years before Elbrus, I had the naive notion that going up was more difficult than coming down. I learned the hard way that the descent can be more grueling. Factor in the fatigue that sets in after several days—it is crucial to stay attentive and cautious. "Never let up when you climb down" is the mantra. It is easy to get lost in the elation of standing on a summit. The feeling of accomplishment is incredibly fulfilling. But it is no time to relax. On the descent, the gravitational field pulls us toward the center of the earth. Consequently, the feet exert an equal and opposite force to keep us upright. The body works harder than usual to compensate, ensuring we don't fall head over heels. On my first expedition to Mount Rainier, I underestimated the amount of energy needed to effectively sustain the descent. I felt fatigued beyond anything I ever imagined and committed to doing better with each expedition. While the climb down can be physically daunting, the mind must stay vigilant to endure the rigor needed to complete the mission. Reaching the summit is a splendid reminder that it is not just a halfway point but time to reenergize for the next leg of the journey. As American mountaineering legend Ed Viesturs writes in his inspiring book *No Shortcuts to the Top*, "Getting to the top is optional. Getting down is mandatory." Given how unpredictable and dangerous climbing can be, I continually remind myself that the goal is not to summit but to get home safely.

While there are thousands of mountains to climb around the world, each varies in degree of difficulty. To keep it simple, mountaineers split climbing into two categories: Technical, like Mount Everest in the Himalayas. Nontechnical, like Kilimanjaro in Tanzania. Technical climbing thus is ascending a mountain using specialized equipment. Since Elbrus falls into the technical camp, we carried a set of tools that can account for the difference between living and dying. Which tool(s) are used and when depends on several factors, including mountain steepness, weather, and terrain conditions. Preparing for a technical climb, essential equipment includes:

1. A harness to secure a climber to a rope or anchor while climbing.

2. Carabiners to keep various pieces of equipment connected to each other. They are oval-shaped spring-loaded clips that act like a lock to keep an object in place.

3. Nylon rope that connects climbers to each other. If a climber falls, someone on the other side of the rope can pull them back up.

4. A belay device that acts as a brake on the rope by applying friction. Along with a climber's "braking hand," it helps to keep tension on the rope as needed.

5. Crampons are traction devices that attach to boots, improving mobility on ice and snow. They are made of aluminum or stainless steel and have up to twelve spikes on the front and bottom. Those spikes dig into the ice to secure the footing.

6. A backpack to carry food, water, clothes, and other gear to safely climb.

Mountaineering is a risky endeavor. Since an accident, avalanche, or stormy weather can occur anytime, it is important to know how and when to use each tool in the kit. While I was technically well-trained, the most important part of my education was learning to self-arrest. This is a technique in which a climber falls and slides down a snow- or ice-covered slope, arresting the slide when not connected to a rope or other belay system. Self-arrest is a skill that can be performed using a combination of boots, hands, and feet. Relying on an ice axe greatly increases the probability of stopping a fall.

When teams start to climb, guides determine along the route when to rope up as a team or proceed solo. If a climber is solo and falls, they self-arrest. If there are at least two climbers connected by a rope, and one of them falls through a crevasse, the falling climber yells as loudly as possible, "Falling." The other climbers immediately drive their ice axes and crampons into the ground and tug on the rope to minimize any distance the climber in distress will fall. The belay device on their harness allows them to adjust the rope's tension. Together they use a combination of tools to pull the climber out of the hole and back on solid footing.

The summit of Mount Elbrus can accommodate dozens of climbers. Since it is flat, teams un-rope, allowing everyone to walk around freely. When ready for the descent, just below the summit, teams rope up again and descend together. Five hundred vertical feet below, our team re-roped and headed down as a unit. Several hours later, at an altitude of 17,000 feet above sea level, we took a break, un-roped, and drank some water. Knowing the next section could be climbed solo, we resumed the descent on our own. The mountain was a gigantic glacier, with most of the terrain covered in ice and snow. Climbing solo meant our ice axes, crampons, and common sense were the tools needed to descend. We were one day away from a shower and a decent meal, feeling great and moving at a healthy clip.

After the break, descending on the same ridge, we climbed solo. Within two minutes, my right foot stepped on an exposed piece of granite. The metal spikes on that crampon quickly scraped the rock, causing me to slip and fall. Since I was on the edge of that ridge, I tumbled feet first, sliding on the steep mountainside in one direction...down...and rapidly. Given all my training, I intuitively activated muscle memory that comes with years of mountaineering. We repeatedly practiced what to do when falling. With the need to self-arrest, I recalled what Mike Bloomberg said when any of his troops were in a bind: "Do what you were trained to do. Don't overthink it and you'll be fine." Mike's words were never so prophetic as at that moment.

Yelling "falling" at the top of my lungs was a survival instinct. I needed to ensure someone on my team heard me. Once I realized what was happening, I stayed calm, keenly aware of the tools needed to self-arrest. Although I was sliding faster than I could have imagined, it felt like a slow-motion scene on a television show. This was an out-of-body experience as I watched myself from high above descend into the abyss. Years of training took over in an instant. With my right hand raised above my shoulder, I drove the ice ax as hard as I could into the mountainside. Slowing the rate of descent, I then nailed my right crampon (with spikes in front) equally hard into the mountain. I repeated the procedure with my left crampon. Quickly, I took stock of where I was in time and space, suspended on the mountain, hanging on for dear life. With an encouraging yell from a voice above, I heard, "Chuck, are you OK?"

"Yes."

"We're coming to get you."

In the interim, my perspective was unlike anything I had ever seen or felt. Lodged six inches from the side of Mount Elbrus, I was connected to this gigantic volcano with one hand and two feet, wondering how I got there. There was nowhere to look but directly into the ice wall that held me captive. The silence of the mountain was deafening, eerily quiet. Suddenly, gripped tightly, waiting to be rescued, I felt stuck on a spectrum between calm and terror. My mind was singularly focused on one thing—don't fall any further. I kept saying to myself, "Hold on." Despite all this, I was fortunate to be gripped to the mountainside amid the world's most beautiful day. The sun was shining, not a cloud in the sky. As I looked to my right, I saw the majestic Caucasus mountains in a way that no photo ever captured. With the glistening white snow, a big yellow sun, and deep blue skies, my composed and confident nature was telling me this would be OK. Getting myself back to reality, I then stared into the ice wall, wondering how this would end.

Out of nowhere, I suddenly started singing *Lose Yourself* by Eminem. Playing like a broken record, over and over.

In what seemed like three long minutes, I heard something coming from above. As I looked up, careful not to dislodge from the mountain, someone was descending. I could not tell who it was, but concluded it was one of our Mountain Madness guides. As he came closer, I saw he was supported by a rope from the team above. Using them as his anchor, he slowly and carefully nudged alongside me. He immediately took a carabiner from his harness and clipped it onto mine. I was now fastened to him, as he was tethered to the team above. As he sensed my anxiousness to climb back to the top of the ridge, with a huge smile, in the most calm and reassuring voice he said,

> *"Chuck...hold on. You're safe now. I'm here. The whole team is patiently waiting for you. No need to rush. Look around. Note the sun. Nice, isn't it? Think about your family, the people back home who love you. Give thought to anyone who made a difference in your life. Breathe. Let it sink in... think about how lucky we are to be here in this moment."*

Feeling renewed and ready to reunite with my mates, my mind reached a point of equanimity. I never experienced a flow state quite like this. As Mihaly Csikszentmihalyi wrote in his insightful book *FLOW: The Psychology of Optimal Experience*, he was "in a state in which people are so involved in an activity that nothing else seems to matter. The experience is so enjoyable that people will continue to do it even at great cost, for the sheer sake of doing it."

My guide was Marc Ripperger. And in that instant, he redefined what it meant to be Emotionally Intelligent. It was the most powerful leadership moment I ever experienced. His Social Awareness...the ability to read the room...me... was unlike anything I had seen in thirty years on Wall Street. Never had I experienced such a teachable moment. All the textbooks, theories, and lessons from the world's greatest CEOs did not half compare to what Marc taught me at that moment. He made me feel like he and I were the only people on earth and brought me to a place that would have made Epictetus and Marcus Aurelius proud.

Marc used every aspect of what would likely be contained in any Stoic philosopher's playbook.

- Accept what is outside of your control; get to work on it.

THE MOMENT THAT DEFINES YOUR LIFE

Epictetus said, "Happiness and freedom begin with a clear understanding of one principle: Some things are within our control, and some things are not. It is only after you have faced up to this fundamental rule and learned to distinguish between what you can and can't control that inner tranquility and outer effectiveness become possible."

Falling off the side of Mount Elbrus was beyond my control. However, the one thing I could control was myself. I "got to work," staying calm with intention, knowing someone up above was coming to get me.

- Focus on the smallest thing you can do right now.

Marcus Aurelius said, "Concentrate every minute like a Roman—like a man—on doing what's in front of you with precise and genuine seriousness, tenderly, willingly, with justice. And on freeing yourself from all other distractions. Yes, you can—if you do everything as if it were the last thing you were doing in your life, and stop being aimless, stop letting your emotions override what your mind tells you, stop being hypocritical, self-centered, irritable."

Zeno spoke directly to me while trying to recover from my fall, "Well-being is realized by small steps, but is truly no small thing." With no shortcuts to the top or bottom of any mountain, all I could do was take one step at a time. Up, down, sideways, it didn't matter. The most important step is the next one. As Rajesh says, "I'm here. Where next?"

- Seek stillness.

Seneca said, "Nothing, to my way of thinking, is a better proof of a well-ordered mind than a man's ability to stop just where he is and pass some time in his own company."

The three minutes I waited for Marc felt like an eternity. However, I found comfort in being alone in my thoughts, having the distinction of being the first and last person on Mount Elbrus to hang from that spot. I was alone but never lonely. I passed the time, hoping one day I would be in a place to help someone hanging on the side of their proverbial mountain.

When climbing, there are standard commands mountaineers use as a protocol to ensure alignment. When Marc was ready to begin the ascent, he spoke in the language we use to communicate actions. Mindful we were ready to proceed, he did a quick equipment check, pulled on the carabiners to confirm our connection, and said, "*Climbing.*" The signal he was ready to climb.

Me: "*Climb on.*" My acknowledgment and subsequent signal for him to advance. I then followed.

As Marc and I ascended toward that ridge, him above, me a body length below, climbing in sync, finding the perfect tempo, my mind snapped into the refrain of Eminem's *Lose Yourself.*

After September 11, 2001, I asked myself a question that continues to pull at me. Did I start climbing to find or lose myself? To this day, I'm not sure. But I am certain this journey of exploration has been a gift beyond my wildest dreams. When engaging in any task, I don't think about the pending achievement anymore. Instead, I commit to giving back that gift each day, one step at a time. I strive each moment to live up to my pledge of going to work daily in the service of someone else's success. The Stoics teach us to focus on effort, not results. To be mindful of doing the small things well. As Marcus Aurelius reminds me every day, "You have to assemble your life action by action."

What happened on 9/11 caused me to rethink my life plan or lack thereof. In an achievement-centric world spinning a few hundred miles per hour, I learned to slow down, take it in, and be present with my thoughts. If I didn't discover anything else on the mountain, that was my best lesson. Thank you, Marc. Any given moment sitting with your thoughts may be the one that changes everything. It is no wonder Marcus Aurelius called his writings *Meditations*. He wrote the twelve books as a source for guidance and self-improvement. Perhaps this book is mine.

As you contemplate your career or life moves, give thought to what happens in those steps. Think of these lessons as tools that help you decide how to decide. Rely on Stoicism and Emotional Intelligence as your equipment. In both subjects, you seek to conclude each moment that is/is not in your control. What happens at those choice points is determined by how you allocate your energy. Is the energy productive and helping you advance on the mountain? Or are you burning it needlessly, losing focus, caught in a spiral of indecision? Like a mountaineer ascending, mindful of the checklist that keeps us climbing, consider what is in my control:

- My thoughts and actions.
- My boundaries.
- Goals I set.
- Where I direct my energy.
- My self-talk.
- How I handle challenges.

What is out of my control:

- The past.
- The future.
- What happens around me.
- The actions of others.
- The opinions of others.
- What others think of me.
- The outcome of my efforts.

Now...sit alone in this moment. Don't overthink it. There is a mountain guide out there waiting to help you find or lose yourself and adapt to life's changing circumstances. Now consider the tools to initiate your climb. Think of them as a mental fortress. You can use a proverbial harness, carabiner, and belay device to connect them all. Or think of them independently. It depends on where you are on the mountain. Consider what Epictetus said, "You become what you give your attention to." If you don't choose what thoughts and images to expose yourself to, someone else will.

I leave you with two questions that most of the world struggles to answer. I hope with the help of Emotional Intelligence and Stoicism, you will close this book and one day answer both.

Who are you?

What do you want?

Now, take a moment and sit with your thoughts. Look around. Think about the people you love and who love you. Look at that shining sun. Nice, isn't it? Ask yourself, "Am I trying to find or lose myself?" Perhaps you don't know but are committed to discovering where it will lead. No matter, the mountains are calling. All they ask is for you to take one step. Do you feel on solid ground? Great, take another. How does it feel? Look around. Think about the people who made a difference in your life. Take another step. What's next?

Climb on!

BIBLIOGRAPHY

Adyashanti. Essay. In *The End of Your World: Uncensored Straight Talk on the Nature of Enlightenment*, 1–2. Boulder, CO: Sounds True, 2010.

"Aretha Franklin." Encyclopædia Britannica. Accessed July 3, 2023. https://www.britannica.com/biography/Aretha-Franklin.

Dattani, Saloni, Lucas Rodés-Guirao, Hannah Ritchie, Max Roser, and Esteban Ortiz-Ospina. "Suicides." Our World in Data, April 2, 2023. https://ourworldindata.org/suicide.

Dobelli, Rolf. "The Art of the Good Life." In *The Art of the Good Life* , 122–25. New York, NY: HATCHETT BOOKS, 2017.

"Figures on Child Sexual Abuse in Germany." UBSKM. Accessed July 3, 2023. https://beauftragte-missbrauch.de/en/themen/definition/figures-on-child-sexual-abuse-in-germany.

George, Alison. "The World's Oldest Paycheck Was Cashed in Beer." New Scientist, June 27, 2016. https://www.newscientist.com/article/2094658-the-worlds-oldest-paycheck-was-cashed-in-beer/.

Litwin, Bob. *Live the best story of your life: A world champion's guide to lasting change.* New York: Hatherleigh, 2016.

"Peter Drucker on the Value of Ignorance." AMA. Accessed July 3, 2023. https://www.amanet.org/articles/peter-drucker-on-the-value-of-ignorance/.

"Peter F. Drucker Claremont Graduate University." Claremont Graduate University, July 19, 2018. https://www.cgu.edu/school/drucker-school-of-management/peter-f-drucker/.

"Prader-Willi Syndrome." Mayo Clinic, January 31, 2018. https://www.mayoclinic.org/diseases-conditions/prader-willi-syndrome/symptoms-causes/syc-20355997.

Pushkar. "Why Do Indian Students Take up Engineering Degrees?" Asian Scientist Magazine, June 2, 2013. https://www.asianscientist.com/2013/06/features/indian-students-engineering-degrees-2013/. [Pushkar is a faculty member at the Department of Humanities and Social Sciences.]

"Sexual Abuse & Assault of Boys & Men: Confidential Support for Men." Sexual Abuse & Assault of Boys & Men | Confidential Support for Men, March 30, 2023. https://1in6.org/.

"Steve Jobs' 2005 Stanford Commencement Address (with Intro by President John Hennessy)." YouTube, May 14, 2008. https://www.youtube.com/watch?v=Hd_ptbiPoXM.

Trusa, Maria. "2." Essay. In *#I Say No More: My Story of Transformation from Abused Girl to Successful Woman*, 46–47. Middletown, DE: Independently published, 2020.

ACKNOWLEDGMENTS

Like climbing a mountain, publishing a book takes time, patience, and a great team. From inception to promotion and all the details in between, the mountaineering mantra applies: Set a goal. One step at a time. Can't do it alone.

Consequently, thank you Steve Carlis and Arestia Rosenberg at 2MarketMedia for helping refine the book idea and introducing me to the publisher. I am grateful to Austin Miller, Debra Englander, and Ashlyn Inman of Post Hill Press for initiating this project and seeing it come to fruition. A special shout out to Barbara Pepe and Taylor Graham of Post Hill for their excellent editing and exquisite attention to detail. Working with the team to complete this project was a pleasure.

Since I spend a lot of time teaching this material, thanks to Chris Whitfield and Gabrielle Previti. Because they have been active participants in many of my college courses, I appreciate their assistance to ensure the words on the page are heard in the same voice as projected in the classroom. To all my students and Climb Leadership clients, thank you for the opportunity to go to work each day in the service of your success.

Thank you especially to Kenny Golde, Bob Litwin, Nirupama Narayanaswamy, Jamie Bassel, Anthony Sicuranza, Uwe Dockhorn, Dominic Dimaria, Maria Trusa, and Rajesh Setty for their friendship and project support. I am blessed they shared their powerful and captivating stories and allowed me the honor to document them in this book.

Finally, a big debt of gratitude to my family for the daily unconditional love and support they provide. I can say with great affection that they are my best teachers.